PUBLISHED IN JUNE 2023

THE TITLE, STYLE OF MAKE-UP AND CONTENTS OF T
ALMANACK ARE STRICTLY COPYRIGHT

Foulsham's Original

OLD MOORE'S
ALMANACK

1697 THE ORIGINAL COPYRIGHT EDITION **2024**

2024 – The Year of New Hope

25 years ago plus, I predicted periods of Revolution in the first quarter of the new Century. To understand this today, the word '*revolution*' includes *major changes* and *disruptions*. In 2024 we will experience another surge in these influences. The year is packed with disruptive, but helpful innovations.

It's a year complicated by world-debt, overhanging everything. Dealing with this issue alongside the UK year and the World's year, I am aware of overlapping timelines. So, while we may have a good time, a severe money problem from elsewhere may surface to worry us.

There are bright influences over the UK this year. Astounding digital tech will be future changing. The last time we were under these influences was in 1997, when Dolly the test tube sheep was created. Today, in healthcare alone, breakthroughs will open lines to personalised medicines and more successful cures. Amazing developments in robotics will open possibilities for us to manufacture again. We will be able to sell at competitive prices to create more jobs. These advances point to better times for us. The UK has strong talents in harnessing Hi-Tech. These new developments will drive a sense of optimism and grow our faith in the future.

With so much disruption at home, we need good leadership to protect us. We need old-fashioned, tried-and-tested rules to manage our challenging future. I am comforted that Pluto in Aquarius and Saturn through Pisces, should steer us to this safe management.

However, we are building serious problems in Wokery! This kind of thought-policing will take us down a spiral to weakness. Wokery too often stands in the way of making the best applicant appointments. Gender and ethnic considerations must not be allowed to lead

© **2023 by OLD MOORE PUBLICATIONS**
Published under Annual Licence by W. Foulsham & Co. Ltd
Printed and bound by CPI Group (UK) Ltd, Croydon, CR0 4YY
News trade distribution by Seymour 020 7429 4000

Tel: (01628) 400600
The Old Barrel Store,
Drayman's Lane,
Marlow, Bucks SL7 2FF

in fulfilling senior appointments. Ability and performance are the only criteria to lead such considerations. I see a growing awareness of this problem building through the year. But not the resolve to correct it.

Throughout the year, Tory party policies and ideas will seem disorganised and out of step, while the country's mood is being influenced towards more compassionate Socialism. I see the beginning of pressures for *change* to local self-governance. I am even concerned for the future of Scotland and Northern Ireland. There will be feelings of anti-Westminster sentiment and Parliament will be forced to give ground to Local Power.

America will be struggling to keep up with its deep financial and social problems. I am expecting some kind of international proposals for a Dollar reset. This may rock our world for a while. I wouldn't be surprised to see Bitcoin becoming a positive *disruptor influence* in this Dollar planning.

In UK, the *protest brigades* will become disturbingly forceful. I expect to see rampant attacks of '*Wokery*'. And more unwanted objections from different groups of '*thought police*'. Annoying though it is, it may turn out well. It should lead us to recognise that we need to legislate to curb *excesses*. We will certainly need to create a zero tolerance of excesses. The UK will grow steadily, while addressing the problems that hold it back. There will be a much stronger focus on the reforms we need. And much more quality thinking, about the way we forge our place in this fast-changing World.

Rishi Sunak, like John Major, came to power under the influence of an eclipse. This was seen as the reason that cut short Major's Premiership. Sunak will test this theory again in 2024. His support from the Conservative Party will be weak, due to faction fighting and confusing policy objectives. While the Labour Party will be bathed by positive influences through the year.

The UK will evolve towards a more caring Society, with the emphasis on shared interests not self-interests. Through the years, I have been disappointed by a decline in our key values. *Truth* has been replaced by *Spin*; meaning lies. *Honesty* and *Integrity* have been swamped by *Fake News*. These faults will attract proper attention this year. People will be expressing their need to get back to the truth.

Highlights to be aware of around the World must include France. The Olympic Games are likely to compete with robust civil unrest and protest movements. Expect a fiery summer. Also, early in the year, France should expect a dramatic scandal. This will involve a high-placed political figure, perhaps even the President himself.

Another revelation I will be looking for is a change of Leadership in Russia. I am trying to make up my mind if this might overlap another important signal this year. The capture and indictment of a war leader.

We are being offered life changing skills that we have shown we are good at. We can build new opportunities for our great country. All we have to do is seize these new opportunities.

I wish you an undisturbed year, Dear Reader, and a sense of calm.

Dr Francis Moore, September 2022

0906 822 9723: *ring Old Moore now* – for the most authentic personal phone horoscope ever made available

Then just tap in your own birth date ... and benefit from the wisdom of the centuries

The uncanny foresight of Britain's No 1 astrologer – focused directly on your own individual birth-chart

Unique personalised reading

There's never been a better way to exploit your personal horoscope opportunities.

Old Moore now has a massive new computer and can produce a personal forecast based on the actual day of your birth. No other astro phone advice service can produce this level of accuracy.

Any day of the week, Old Moore can update you on the planetary influences which surround you and point up the opportunities which will be open to you.

Unique record of prediction

The principles of astro interpretation laid down by Old Moore have proved amazingly reliable and accurate. That's how the Almanack continues to astound the world, year after year. And that's how Old Moore can analyse your own personal world.

PS: phone today and see what you should be looking out for.

Meet Old Moore any day

For just 60p per minute you can hear this authoritative overview of your life, work and happiness. Not the usual 'fortune-telling' patter. But enlightened insights into how best to exploit the day and the *moment*.

Remember, unlike any other phone astrologer, Old Moore will ask you for the *day, month and year* of your birth, to give you the most individual advice and predictions ever possible.

So touch hands with the immortal Old Moore. Ring this number and get a truly personalised forecast, from the world's most acclaimed astrologer.

0906 822 9723

Calls cost 60p per minute at all times.
(Charges may be higher for payphones and non-BT networks.)
Complaints & Service Provider (ATS): 0844 836 9769

2024 – World Preview

GREAT BRITAIN AND WORLD ECONOMY

In keeping with Old Moore's theme of improvement, the UK chart shows the economy slowly growing in 2024, although perhaps at less than one per cent. 2024 is likely to see the stock markets rally. The planetary picture for the New York stock exchange shows high confidence from May with Earnings per Share growing by as much as 12 per cent. Predictive charts show the UK property market stagnating but not collapsing; expect some improvement late in the year.

The Tory government may be in crisis with a general election looming. Rishi Sunak became PM on 25 October 2022, the exact day of an eclipse. This signals that the Conservative leadership this year must negotiate unexpected chaos and controversy. The 2024 Tory party chart nevertheless indicates a government that really believes it can put things right and deliver: they may increase spending in some public sectors, be more conciliatory and ready to listen to the public. However, there are signs of division, factions and confused loyalties *within* the party. Healing these will not prove easy, and may be marred by scandal. The Tory chart suggests the best time to call an election in 2024 is late March or late April when enabling Jupiter is prominent. Interestingly, Labour's birth chart has an alignment of planets involving the dynamic Sun, pushy Mars, lucky Jupiter and powerful Pluto which bring support and strength in 2024.

UNITED STATES

Predictive charts for the USA in 2024 show that the uncertainty surrounding the economy will settle and overall growth will get back to pre-pandemic rates. Even so, financial pressures with the Jupiter–Saturn alignment in August could disillusion those hoping for lower interest rates. The first half of the year shows potential flare ups with other countries, possibly China, as the latter seeks to expand its own powers. In the latter half of 2024, a Pluto–Mercury configuration shows the USA is in no mood for compromise.

The focus of interest will be the US Presidential Election, which will be a judgement on President Biden's economic policies. The chart of the Democrats is laced with tension and infighting in 2024, possibly with individuals speaking out against the President. As for Joe Biden himself, he may have overestimated his own popularity and the election may be a close-run thing. Elsewhere, Donald Trump's solar return chart this year shows Saturn and Neptune close to the MC – not a good augur for public goodwill or probity, and evidence shows that his bedrock of support may be on the wane. He may begin to doubt himself, as other candidates come to the fore and race ahead.

EUROPE

Chancellor Olaf Scholz's three-party coalition in Germany is a bullish entity, reflected in its decision to rebuild its military as Ukraine was attacked in 2022. One major astrological indication shows Germany is ready to undertake sweeping reform of the economy, but unpopular social measures may surface around late March and late July. Economic improvement in exports provides some light at the end of the tunnel, but more ordinary Germans will be voicing their disapproval. France will see robust conflicts – expect civil unrest and protest movements as Macron's popularity falters during April's eclipse and the Jupiter–Uranus conjunction. There are further stresses on France's chart from fiery Mars during summer at the time of the Paris Olympics (26 July to 11 August) when security forces need to be extra vigilant. There are signs of a major scandal involving a high-placed political figure in early 2024, perhaps Macron himself. On a positive note, there will be strong support for the Ukraine leader Volodymyr Zelensky across Europe. Peace talks early in the year might look promising but any optimism could soon be dashed by actual events in Ukraine.

ISRAEL

Last year, Old Moore suggested a return for Benjamin Netanyahu, and this he did when he assumed power for a fifth term in November 2022. This is in a coalition forged with parties said to be the most right-wing yet. As such, there may be striking workers in the news in April. Further street protests are indicated from May onwards in response to unpopular political reforms. The Moon is opposite Pluto which is an aspect of oppression. It therefore appears that little is likely to change for Israel's neighbours in Palestine.

RUSSIA AND CHINA

The vote of no confidence from the West for Russia and China continues. At the time of writing, the war on Ukraine shows no sign of a conclusion. Putin's decision to invade Ukraine is something of a gamble that he now feels he must win, and in January there may be surprises in store. Russia's chart depicts solidarity through allies, especially China where Xi Jinping's support will be more public. Putin's chart shows he may also have to contend with unexpected political rivalry in 2024, though supportive Jupiter bodes well for him in the Presidential elections in March–April.

China's economy has been steadily growing but will it be a powerhouse in 2024? The main concern for the West is the autocratic leader, Xi Jinping. This year, China's chart shows the President may take one step too far with economic reforms and ongoing hostility towards countries in the Asia–Pacific area. Slowing economic growth may be the reality in 2024, and unpopular oppressive measures on neighbouring countries in February may even invoke economic sanctions in March, denting its export drive.

HM King Charles III

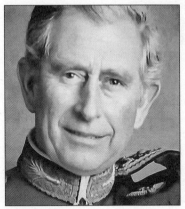

© Welsh Snapper/Alamy Stock Photo

When Queen Elizabeth II, at age 96, sadly passed away on 8 September 2022, her firstborn son, Charles Philip Arthur George, automatically became King Charles III of the United Kingdom. He was crowned at his Coronation on Saturday 6 May at exactly 12.02 pm under an intense media spotlight, alongside his Queen consort, Camilla. It would be true to say that there had been some foreboding in the air for months, with some astrologers forecasting that the Coronation would not proceed as planned, or possibly would not even proceed at all; worse, that Charles would not rule as monarch. Some suggested that he'd hand over the reins to his son, Prince William, instead. Perhaps these astrologers may have had in mind the presence of erratic, rebellious Uranus, whose influence is often toward sudden, unexpected change, and which is shown on the Coronation chart as conjunct the Sun (rulership) and opposite the Moon (the public). But the main reason for these unfavourable omens was the lunar eclipse on 5 May, less than 24 hours before the Coronation. The eclipse in astrology can indeed disturb the smooth running of an institution and can even hamper it from getting off the ground.

However, Old Moore can point to many examples of individuals who have assumed public roles at the time of an eclipse and where things *have* gone on to run as planned. What may happen in these instances, is that the person's period in office throws up surprises, even shocks. For example, Ronald Reagan who assumed the American presidency on an eclipse, was the target of an attempted assassination but his Presidency is generally viewed as successful. And while Edward VIII acceded to the throne on 20 January 1936 (around the time of an eclipse) and was soon to abdicate, his successor George VI began his reign on 11 December 1936, even *closer* to an eclipse but with no subsequent controversies. What the 5 May eclipse might signify, therefore, are some unorthodox events for King Charles's reign, mostly *of his own making.*

The King was born on 14 November 1948 at 9.14 pm, in Buckingham Palace, which gives him the Sun in secretive, intense Scorpio and the Moon in earthy Taurus. The rising sign is dignified, proud Leo, but despite this often theatrical ascendant, King Charles is a man of subtlety, secrecy, passion and dignity, with all of the hallmarks of water-sign sympathy for others – something that is not often remarked upon. Transformative Pluto is prominent in his chart and reminds him of his enormous potential power to effect change, and the importance of public opinion.

For a rounded picture of the King, it is important to compare his chart against that of his Queen, Camilla. The new Queen was born on 17 July 1947 at 7.10 am, with both the Sun and Moon in maternal, sympathetic Cancer. The Leo ascendant brings a sense of pride and dignity (something shared with Charles) and a toughness, along with a need for approval and respect. Her first house (personality) is affected by authoritarian Saturn–Pluto (a conjunction), reminding her that she lives in a world of strict rules and responsibility imposed by others, and can never forget it. Venus in Cancer signifies the mother-instinct in personal relationships, whilst Mars in Gemini indicates that her preference is for a partner who is articulate, witty and intellectual.

The Composite chart, which is a chart of the relationship itself, gives us an astrological x-ray view inside it. Charles and Camilla's shows Composite Saturn in the First house, which puts a limit on how much the relationship can be freely expressed to the world. Also, the Composite Venus–Saturn conjunction indicates that despite strong feelings for each other, duty and protocol may intervene so that the relationship must be put on hold. Even so, the presence of earthy Saturn (the Lord of Time) is also a good augur for durability – each partner feels safe and deeply comfortable with the other.

One major predictive chart for 2024 suggests communication problems among the family, or even PR difficulties and a waning in popularity, shown on the 'relationship house' of the Coronation chart. In 2024, with the Sun and fiery Mars conjunct in opposition to wilful, freedom-loving Uranus, Charles may surprise people by being more boldly, publicly assertive about issues close to his heart than many believe a King has a right to be. Most of 2024's predictive charts are dominated by Uranus, which may mean that Charles will no longer embrace a position in his mother's shadow but move free from it. However, the year begins with duty-bound Saturn in January showing him limitations he'd rather not face. Throughout August, intense Pluto is aspecting his natal Moon (domestic issues) and the power of the past looms – emotional power conflicts with family members may arise. On the lighter side, he is ready to throw off certain shackles.

The overall planetary picture in 2024 suggests that King Charles may be content to let others do the thinking for him, and sit back a little, as it were, in his constitutional role as monarch. If Charles's reign as King, influenced by the timing of his Coronation, begins to look rather unconventional then we may see this only increase, possibly during the second half of 2024, from July. This is when the progressed Midheaven (public image) conjuncts erratic Uranus. Announcements regarding his constitutional role as King may be forthcoming. Charles may simply want more personal freedom – and he may be ready to break with protocol in one way or another to get it. Until now, he may have felt hampered in his ambitions to change the world for the better, now we should prepare to see more of his input into modern society and its institutions, in surprising ways, too.

Anton Du Beke

© Francis Knight/Alamy Stock Photo

Anton Du Beke is a television presenter, singer, writer and – above all – a professional ballroom dancer. For the last two seasons he has been a judge on the hugely popular BBC show *Strictly Come Dancing*, moving him up from his previous role as a professional partner of a celebrity dancer in each series of the show since its inception. Anton's easy-going style and sense of humour has brought him a solid fan base and television stardom far from the world of ballroom dancing.

Anton Du Beke, whose birth name was Anthony Paul Beke was born on 20 July 1966 in Sevenoaks, Kent. Du Beke has an international heritage, with a Hungarian father and a Spanish mother; he was born with the Sun, Mars and Jupiter all in the zodiac sign of Cancer, which ensured him of a sensitive and caring nature. His overall astrological profile indicates great physical stamina allied to solid endurance.

By usual standards, Anton came relatively late to ballroom dancing and did not take his first lessons until the age of 14. By 17, he had decided that dancing would be his career and by dint of natural talent, aided by Mercury in Leo and Venus in Gemini, he gradually amassed the skills to add to his determination to become a professional dancer. With the Moon in Leo, and no doubt a very strong rising sign (which sadly we cannot know without his time of birth), Anton Du Beke matches tenacity with a great sense of humour, artistic prowess and a determination never to give in to physical or mental weakness. On the way he has not allowed his own steady rise to stardom to stand in the way of an overriding compassion that is the hallmark of his astrological makeup.

Du Beke is married with two children and with all his Cancerian planetary positions and the strength of them in his natal chart he is clearly a family man who understands the importance of a settled home life. Again, typically of his astrological chart, Anton makes strong and enduring friendships and enjoys general popularity.

One of the hallmarks of this particular birth chart is variety. This is a well spread chart which indicates that Anton is likely to take on new challenges in the future. We could see him in acting roles, and it looks likely that as the years go on, he will write more books, possibly not simply the novel type for which he is already known. There is virtually no limit to the ways in which such a versatile character will exercise himself and we can expect to see his name appearing in ways that could be both delightful and surprising. This is a man whose talents appear limitless, and we can expect to see him making further use of them.

Adele

© Doug Peters/Alamy Stock Photo

It goes without saying that Adele is a living phenomenon: she's one of the biggest-selling female recording artists in the world, with sales topping 100 million records. After the release of her second album, *21*, in 2011, Adele shot to superstardom – and the rest, as the old cliché has it, is history. *21* is currently the *world's* biggest-selling album of the 21st century. It has earned her multiple citations in the *Guinness Book of Records*. The year after its release saw Adele selected to write the theme song for the James Bond film *Skyfall*, garnering her an Academy Award and Golden Globe Award for Best Original Song. Alongside her string of musical awards, Adele also became an MBE in 2013. So, it must be asked, what comes next?

Adele Laurie Blue Adkins was born on 5 May 1988 in London at 8.19 am. She has the Sun in sensuous, down-to-earth Taurus; 'everything is about authenticity with her', as one of her aides once remarked. She also has a sensitive, emotional, home-loving Cancerian ascendant. The Sagittarian Moon (hope, optimism, idealism, a need to believe) is caught up with erratic Uranus, strict Saturn and dreamy Neptune. This means sudden attractions and passions that can quickly dissipate and a need for freedom from emotional constraints. While Saturn in her seventh house means she'll take relationship commitments very seriously, Uranus's simultaneous need for freedom means there's a dichotomy that she will have to work out.

Overall, Adele needs to come to terms with her own power and sense of independence. The Sun and expansive Jupiter opposing powerful Pluto indicates ambition, a dreamer of big dreams, always seeking to grow and expand horizons, but also a generosity of spirit. She has the capacity to literally change the lives of others, too – and in the larger scheme of things wants to be a force for good in the world.

2024 (certainly after May) looks likely to be a year in which Adele will find it difficult to settle, whether on an emotional level (as an issue from the past comes calling) or domestically. She may find it beneficial to be flexible about her personal and home life. The influence of unstable, impatient Uranus may make her at times prone to emotional whims and changes of direction, so much so that others feel they can't keep up with her. With Venus conjunct Chiron on her birth chart, her relationships are always serious, learning experiences; there may be another on the way as the year begins. However, with the Jupiter return in March, her career will simply go from strength to unprecedented strength, with expanded opportunities and big plans for the summer – although she must make sure her goals are achievable. Some might say that with her chart, anything is achievable for Adele!

200-year Perpetual Calendar

Do you know on which day of the week you or your friends were born? You may remember that World War II was declared on Sunday, 3 September 1939, but on which day did World War I start?

    This calendar, created originally by C. E. Forsythe, allows you to find the weekday for any date from 1850 to 2050. You will find it useful and informative and very simple to use. Just follow the instructions to check birthdays, events and special occasions.

- Find the year in Table A.
- Follow across on the same line to Table B and select the number under the relevant month.
- Add this number to the date.
- Look up this number in Table C and follow across to the left to find the day of the week.

Table A / **Table B**

								Jan	Feb	Mar	Apri	May	June	July	Aug	Sept	Oct	Nov	Dec
1850	1878		1918	1946	1974	2002	2030	2	5	5	1	3	6	1	4	0	2	5	0
1851	1879		1919	1947	1975	2003	2031	3	6	6	2	4	0	2	5	1	3	6	1
* 1852	1880		1920	1848	1976	2004	2032	4	0	1	4	6	2	4	0	3	5	1	3
1853	1881		1921	1949	1977	2005	2033	6	2	2	5	0	3	5	1	4	6	2	4
1854	1882		1922	1950	1978	2006	2034	0	3	3	6	1	4	6	2	5	0	3	5
1855	1883		1923	1951	1979	2007	2035	1	4	4	0	2	5	0	3	6	1	4	6
* 1856	1884		1924	1952	1980	2008	2036	2	5	6	2	4	0	2	5	1	3	6	1
1857	1885		1925	1953	1981	2009	2037	4	0	0	3	5	1	3	6	2	4	0	2
1858	1886		1926	1954	1982	2010	2038	5	1	1	4	6	2	4	0	3	5	1	3
1859	1887		1927	1955	1983	2011	2039	6	2	2	5	0	3	5	1	4	6	2	4
* 1860	1888		1928	1956	1984	2012	2040	0	3	4	0	2	5	0	3	6	1	4	6
1861	1889	1901	1929	1957	1985	2013	2041	2	5	5	1	3	6	1	4	0	2	5	0
1862	1890	1902	1930	1958	1986	2014	2042	3	6	6	2	4	0	2	5	1	3	6	1
1863	1891	1903	1931	1959	1987	2015	2043	4	0	0	3	5	1	3	6	2	4	0	2
* 1864	1892	1904	1932	1960	1988	2016	2044	5	1	2	5	0	3	5	1	4	6	2	4
1865	1893	1905	1933	1961	1989	2017	2045	0	3	3	6	1	4	6	2	5	0	3	5
1866	1894	1906	1934	1962	1990	2018	2046	1	4	4	0	2	5	0	3	6	1	4	6
1867	1895	1907	1935	1963	1991	2019	2047	2	5	5	1	3	6	1	4	0	2	5	0
* 1868	1896	1908	1936	1964	1992	2020	2048	3	6	0	3	5	1	3	6	2	4	0	2
1869	1897	1909	1937	1965	1993	2021	2049	5	1	1	4	6	2	4	0	3	5	1	3
1870	1898	1910	1938	1966	1994	2022	2050	6	2	2	5	0	3	5	1	4	6	2	4
1871	1899	1911	1939	1967	1995	2023		0	3	3	6	1	4	6	2	5	0	3	5
* 1872		1912	1940	1968	1996	2024		1	4	5	1	3	6	1	4	0	2	5	0
1873		1913	1941	1969	1997	2025		3	6	6	2	4	0	2	5	1	3	6	1
1874		1914	1942	1970	1998	2026		4	0	0	3	5	1	3	6	2	4	0	2
1875		1915	1943	1971	1999	2027		5	1	1	4	6	2	4	0	3	5	1	3
* 1876		1916	1944	1972	2000	2028		6	2	3	6	1	4	6	2	5	0	3	5
1877	1900	1917	1945	1973	2001	2029		1	4	4	0	2	5	0	3	6	1	4	6

Table C

Sunday	1	8	15	22	29	36
Monday	2	9	16	23	30	37
Tuesday	3	10	17	24	31	
Wednesday	4	11	18	25	32	
Thursday	5	12	19	26	33	
Friday	6	13	20	27	34	
Saturday	7	14	21	28	35	

Example: 3 March 1896
March 1896 = 0
Date = 3
0 + 3 = 3 so it fell on a Tuesday

Example: 27 July 2005
July 2005 = 5
Date = 27
5 + 27 = 32 so it will fall on a Wednesday

* Years on the lines to the right of the asterisks are leap years.

Volodymyr Zelensky

One of the more unlikely figures to tread the world stage as a war leader is Volodymyr Zelensky, the Ukraine president whose country was invaded in February 2022. He's been lauded for his courage and never-say-die spirit, but he himself tends to downplay his personal qualities. In the meantime, Putin has suffered major setbacks as a result of the resilience of Ukraine's militias. Is Zelensky the man to defeat him? Volodymyr Zelensky was, after all, not groomed for political life – he's a former comedian and actor. 'I remember his first days when he just became the president, he was very sensitive', says one colleague. 'Zelensky soon learned that leadership was pitiless ... And it took him some time to harden himself'. Certainly, he's ambitious, and he is now certain to fulfil his own

© SOPA Images/Alamy Stock Photo

stated ambition to go down in history. But what kind of a man is he underneath?

Volodymyr Zelenskyy was born on 25 January 1978 (incidentally the name Zelenskyy, with its double 'y' iteration is the true Ukrainian spelling – it's on his passport). He has Sun in humanitarian Aquarius, Moon in showy, proud Leo and an airy, quick-thinking, inquisitive Gemini ascendant. With do-it-big Jupiter conjunct the ascendant he is generous, optimistic, liberal, tolerant and possesses a great sense of humour – but with a definite need for self-aggrandizement! This is the hallmark of attention-seeking Moon in Leo, but Zelensky also tends to over-idealise others to the point where relationships may ultimately be a let-down. This is the work of Neptune, which blinds him to the faults of others. This may be why some have questioned his capability as a war leader. Still, the Sun opposite Mars adds a sense of urgency and competitiveness – certain gung-ho tendencies will have to be reined in – and although dispassionate he is not, he might lack the strategic skills of a good general.

The crucial 'part of fortune' on his descendant (relationships) shows that whatever Zelensky does this year, success cannot be gained by mere ambition. Military triumph and progress can only be achieved through diplomacy and give-and-take. Of course, it's also going to be a rocky road and with shady Pluto and unstable Uranus at large in February and March, we may see him being wrongfooted in some way – it may be a phase when things suddenly seem to fall apart. Whether or not the war has reached a conclusion, April and May are his best months for any personal advantage or breakthrough, but this could also be temporary, too, and overconfidence (perhaps one of his failings) must be avoided. Astrological indications show that the best chance of resolving conflict in any lasting sense might be around the time of the eclipse on 2 October 2024, when enabling Jupiter begins a new cycle of personal growth through his birth chart.

Ukraine, Russia and the West – Where Will It All End?

It's the war everyone is talking about: the one with the maverick leader whose country has been invaded, the one that has seen a huge humanitarian response in Britain and other European countries, the one that has even affected our gas bills in the UK. It was heralded by a lengthy Russian military build-up that had been brewing since early 2021, when Vladimir Putin wanted to stop his neighbour from joining NATO. Then, in early 2022 the Russian premier announced a military operation in eastern Ukraine and the missiles soon started to land upon the capital Kyiv, too. Russia's invasion began on 24 February 2022, at around 5 am UCT co-ordinated Universal Time). The president of Ukraine, Volodymyr Zelensky sprang into action, enforcing martial law, and preparing for war. But when might we see an end to this conflict? Will there be the resolve around Europe to provide the strength that Zelensky needs if he is to be the victor? And what will be its lasting impact on the West?

The predictions from experts at the time of writing is far from optimistic. Commentators offer many different scenarios and theories on how it could all end, including the Russian offensive succeeding; a Ukrainian breakthrough that gets Putin to the negotiating table; or a leadership change in Russia. Some even predict a kind of stalemate where the war proceeds indefinitely. No doubt, it will prove costly, both in terms of money and of human life and it does not look likely to be ending any time soon. The latter of these scenarios is what the experts focus on, some on the fact that supplies of ammunition – being donated by Ukraine's supporters in the West – are not inexhaustible. But what does the astrology tell us?

When we look at the time of the invasion, the 'birth chart' reliably shows Mars, God of war, closely aligned with Pluto, God of destruction and death. And it's no surprise that Mars is also placed sensitively on a predictive chart for the day of the anniversary of the invasion in February 2024, indicating that the conflict has yet more time to run. The conjunction of Jupiter and Uranus in March 2024 suggests one side having a significant advantage over the other, yet later in the month both countries seemingly become entrenched. On the birth chart for Ukraine, powerful Pluto is significantly located on the MC – a planet that's always a political force to be reckoned with on a national chart. The Sun is in Leo, and hardy, resilient and ambitious Capricorn is on the ascendant, all of which reveal Ukraine to be self-confident, proud and no longer a country that can be owned or easily pushed around by foreign aggressors.

The birth chart for Russia reveals aggressive Mars and erratic Uranus in the house of partners/open enemies, as we may have expected. Significantly, in 2024 hardliner Saturn begins moving through the house of diplomacy/open enemies which portends major difficulties in international relationships generally. An entrenched, stubborn position in any possible future negotiations is therefore indicated. However, in 2024 one of Russia's predictive charts clearly shows strength through the support of its allies, especially China which is, after all, its biggest trade partner. This is in spite of the fact that another chart – for late 2023 – shows massive pressure with the Sun opposite natal Saturn. What *does* stand out in 2024 is an alignment between the progressed MC and the ascendant of the birth chart. This is extremely important – it's suggested that in early 2024 Russia *secretly* wishes to see an end to the conflict (the MC symbolises things coming to a conclusion). Might this be due to increased pressure from all sides, national and international?

WILL THERE BE A BREAKTHROUGH?

Transits to Ukraine's chart see some of the worst difficulties and flashpoints in late 2023 and early 2024 with taskmaster Saturn and unpredictable Uranus involved mid-October, mid to late November through early December. Ordinarily we'd expect Jupiter to ease the pressure and point to a solution; but this is no ordinary situation, and we can't be hard and fast with predictions. However, enabling Jupiter makes a series of alignments to planets on the Ukraine chart (in close succession) from early April 2024 until late May. Significant dates (where Ukraine's fortunes seem to be improving) would be close to the 2nd, 14th and 23rd April, and the 5th, 8th, 9th 18th and 30th May. These may represent Ukraine's best chance at some kind of military advantage – but that is all. It could simply represent a false dawn whereby things improve only temporarily, thus stimulating overconfidence for Ukraine.

The personal charts of the leaders cannot be ignored either. I note with interest that these Jupiter contacts are also mirrored in Volodymyr Zelensky's own chart between late March and late June 2024 – could this mean that the Ukraine leader will have something to feel pleased about? Vladimir Putin has a Jupiter return (the planet of opportunity) in April 2024 which moves through his seventh house of international relations for twelve months. The best chance of *resolution* indicated by astrology – as opposed to victory by either side – is in October 2024 with the solar eclipse in Libra (the peacemaker). If this doesn't happen, there's still light at the end of the tunnel on the invasion chart as Jupiter (the enabler) crosses into the seventh house, that of 'friends and enemies', although this does not occur until August 2025.

Most pundits agree that this war could go on for years, as Russia seeks to engage the West in a protracted proxy war that will deplete the energies of Ukraine's allies, both politically and militarily. As we've seen, the broad astrological picture seems to bear this out.

Your 2024 Birthday Guide

By working with the major astrological influences, you can take control and give your life a better focus. These personal guides show you how to make the most of the positive times and also indicate which days need to be handled with care.

ARIES BORN PEOPLE
Birthdays: 21 March to 20 April inclusive
Planet: Mars. Birthstone: Diamond. Lucky day: Tuesday

Keynote for the Year: *The first half of the year offers a good chance of financial gain, but much of the twelve months may see you learning major lessons from the past.*

JANUARY: MAIN TRENDS: 9–10 You have the knack of getting your plans to turn out just right – the bigger the plan, the better as helpful influences surround your professional life. **11–13** The optimum time to trust your intuition – things will be on the up. **19–20** Loved ones play a significant role in your life; in particular, an old relationship may take on extra significance. **KEY DATES: HIGHS 16–17** Capitalise on any unexpected good luck. **LOWS 3–5** If the road ahead looks rocky and your progress is slow, go easy on yourself.

FEBRUARY: MAIN TRENDS: 4–5 Give up anything that's no longer fulfilling and, above all, be clear in your own mind about your financial future. **17–18** The planetary focus is on your personal life – partnerships may bring rewards, and frank discussion can dispel worries. **19–20** A community-based matter proves enjoyable – there may even be new friendships on the horizon. **KEY DATES: HIGHS 13–14** Go straight for what you really want and be spontaneous in your thoughts and actions! **LOWS 1; 27–28** You may lack the willpower to work hard so take some time out to rest, if possible.

MARCH: MAIN TRENDS: 2–3 Don't overreact if life doesn't go your way. You may benefit from spending some time contemplating spiritual matters. **20–21** Be patient if an issue in a relationship requires resolving. **23–24** The Sun moves into your sign and vitality and love of life are in the ascendant – there is little you can't achieve with some positive thinking. **KEY DATES: HIGHS 12–13** Stand on your own two feet, take care of business and you may create positive opportunities. **LOWS 25–26** Accept that there are some things you have no power to change. There's wisdom in letting things be.

APRIL: MAIN TRENDS: 6–7 Venus moves into your sign, so you can expect personal relationships to be fulfilling. **15–17** Prepare for a setback in your primary ambition; however, you may have some success where you least expect it. **20–21** Practical matters go your way, and you may find you are rather better off than you thought. **KEY DATES: HIGHS 8–9** These days will see you get the best from life and the personal satisfaction of having your efforts recognised. **LOWS 22–23** Take a methodical approach to practical matters and don't worry if you are delayed.

MAY: MAIN TRENDS: 1–2 Don't be afraid to be a little ruthless if you need to dispense with something that isn't working or is holding you back. **10–11** Your social life is extremely pleasant, and your relationship is fulfilling under these trends. **21–22** Communication is positively highlighted, leading to valuable new information. A negotiation may go your way. **KEY DATES: HIGHS 5–6** At work, a superior may support your ambitions, or you may receive a promotion of some kind. **LOWS 19–20** Be patient regarding any setbacks, you will reach your satisfying conclusion in the end.

JUNE: MAIN TRENDS: 5–7 Your ruling planet, Mars, is in your sign so you can burn the candle at both ends. Beware of interfering in other people's business. **12–13** A great time for family gatherings.

Personal pursuits, especially centred around the home, are apt to be highly rewarding. **20–21** Communication and negotiation is positively highlighted – be on the lookout for new information related to a professional or business interest. **KEY DATES: HIGHS 2–3; 30** An important period when it comes to sowing the seeds of future success. **LOWS 15–17** Be aware that you may temporarily struggle to keep things organised and on an even keel.

JULY: MAIN TRENDS: 1–2 Give careful consideration to a present course of professional action – try to keep a cool head if things go wrong. **21–22** A beneficial trend is operating in the sphere of love and romance, possibly increasing your attractiveness. **23–24** Go with the flow if career changes take place and take decisive action when needed. **KEY DATES: HIGHS 26–27** Beneficial planetary positions bring you plenty of good ideas – put some into practice. **LOWS 13–14** Pay attention to small details in every sense but prepare for a few unavoidable mishaps.

AUGUST: MAIN TRENDS: 1–3 A cautious financial approach may be required; take a close look at your budget before spending unnecessarily. **17–18** Work should be enjoyable and successful; you may get the chance to rise above your competition. **20–21** Work matters continue to improve, making this an excellent time for completing projects or advancing with business initiatives. **KEY DATES: HIGHS 22–23** Life should be going your way now, so consider pushing your luck just a little. **LOWS 9–10** Keep everyday life as simple and uncomplicated as possible during this short low patch, Aries.

SEPTEMBER: MAIN TRENDS: 3–4 If you struggle with a practical matter, take an impartial standpoint and don't let other people's emotions affect you. **11–12** Money is favourably highlighted in your chart so this could turn out to be a fairly profitable period, with positive influences also surrounding business and emotional involvements. **22–23** Your personal life is fulfilling as you strike a good balance between heart and mind. **KEY DATES: HIGHS 19–20** Broaden your intellectual and social interests at this time and you may experience a little good fortune. **LOWS 5–7** Put big ideas and plans on the back burner at this time.

OCTOBER: MAIN TRENDS: 8–9 Play to your strengths at work and use your initiative and leadership skills. You should see rewards. **10–11** Trends bring you clear insight and perspective on an important matter; a good time for a frank discussion. Travel is also positively highlighted. **23–24** Take time to build up new ideas and plans and avoid any tendency to rush into things. **KEY DATES: HIGHS 16–17** Be ready for whatever comes your way. You will thrive on a certain amount of change. **LOWS 2–4** You may be feeling a little over-sensitive so step back a little if you can and rest.

NOVEMBER: MAIN TRENDS: 1–2 Trends increase your overall popularity – take the chance to impress people in conversation and communicate with others on new levels. **5–6** It's not what you know, but who you know – this applies especially at work right now. **22–23** You may hear something inspirational, especially if you're able to expand your mind through travel and cultural pursuits. **KEY DATES: HIGHS 13–14** You have certain competitive advantages now which may help your career ambitions. **LOWS 26–27** Trends reduce your power to influence situations, so avoid any risky decisions.

DECEMBER: MAIN TRENDS: 1–2 As the festive season begins, your chart favours social outings – you may make new friends. **15–16** You intend to stand out from the crowd but take care not to allow your enthusiasm to come across as overbearing. **21–22** Professionally you'll be popular and should find you can get your own way easily. **KEY DATES: HIGHS 10–11** The right time to set new ideas in motion, the bigger, the better! **LOWS 23–24** A somewhat lacklustre run up to Christmas this year but this won't be disappointing if you enjoy a cosy time at home.

TAURUS BORN PEOPLE
Birthdays: 21 April to 21 May inclusive
Planet: Venus. Birthstone: Emerald. Lucky day: Friday

Keynote for the Year: *A year when you can make successful fresh starts in almost any area, though a long-term friendship may present you with some challenges.*

JANUARY: MAIN TRENDS: 1–2 Your personal charm, with all its uplifting energies, sees you warmly welcomed in most situations. **14–15** Prepare for some highly emotional conversations – trends indicate that someone may tell you some home truths. Put pride to one side and think honestly about what's being said. **27–28** Trends assist your powers of persuasion, leading to productive talks with influential professional people. **KEY DATES: HIGHS 19–20** Favourable influences surround you in your career or your personal relationships. **LOWS 6–7** Take care over decision-making as your judgement may be a little clouded.

FEBRUARY: MAIN TRENDS: 4–5 You need to feel free so find something new and interesting to do. Don't take any travel plans for granted. **11–12** Your chart shows a real prospect of advancement, especially by working in a partnership. Take the long view and don't lose faith. **22–23** Meetings and conversations with powerful people could be agreeable. Keep your main priorities in mind. **KEY DATES: HIGHS 15–16** If other people's plans don't suit you, move ahead and make your own. **LOWS 2–3; 29** Prepare for setbacks and delays to projects; don't expect too smooth a ride, but don't be beaten too easily.

MARCH: MAIN TRENDS: 4–5 Although your tastes may be a little extravagant, explore new avenues to maximise your material resources and enjoy more of the good life! **15–17** Communication is easy, and you benefit from meeting new people and exchanging ideas; a great time to make new friends. **22–23** With boundless energy and good judgement, you seem to have a solution to every problem – especially in the professional sphere. **KEY DATES: HIGHS 13–14** Get ready to succeed with new projects when life offers you the chance. And it will! **LOWS 1–2; 27–29** You may find it difficult to get your own way; focus on simple tasks.

APRIL: MAIN TRENDS: 5–6 Trends focus on your personal qualities. You are keen to accommodate others and bring out the best in them. **16–18** You are enjoying feeling attractive to others. Consider looking for exciting social opportunities that may also fulfil your urge for freedom. **20–21** With the Sun in your sign, you may receive a little good luck in your moves towards your ambitions. You never know what big favours you may receive if you ask. **KEY DATES: HIGHS 10–11** Don't be afraid to go for what you want but listen to your hunches about others. **LOWS 24–25** You may feel lacking in energy and stamina – this is a temporary lull so don't worry.

MAY: MAIN TRENDS: 2–3 Kick back and be content with your efforts thus far. A sense of gratitude for your life can bring positive experiences if you did but know it! **9–10** On a practical level, certain issues at home may require careful thought. Avoid the tendency to be a know-all. **25–26** Your strength now lies in money-making, indeed, financially, this may prove a stable period, allowing you to plan ahead properly. **KEY DATES: HIGHS 7–8** The planetary picture indicates a very successful period for personal relationships. **LOWS 21–22** Be objective in your attitude if your views seem out of step with others.

JUNE: MAIN TRENDS: 5–6 At work, or in anything competitive, your superior judgement and accurate decision-making will stand you in good stead. **18–19** Trust your instincts and allow yourself to enjoy your current high profile; it seems to confirm your popularity. **21–22** Trends favour practical matters, especially those with money-making potential. Financial dreams may be realised but it is essential to take professional advice before making any decisions. **KEY DATES: HIGHS 3–4** A combination of effort and luck should enable you to make the most of this forward-looking influence. **LOWS 17–19** Don't fixate on how to achieve certain goals or be too attached to their outcomes right now.

JULY: MAIN TRENDS: 11–13 Some plans that are on the drawing board may only get so far before hitting a snag. You'll have to work harder to accomplish your objectives so it may be time to suspend certain activities. **9–10** Joint endeavours, whether business or pleasure, move in a positive vein, especially if you recognise the importance of give and take. **22–23** Domestic activities may prove rewarding and intimate conversations with family or friends are helpful and reassuring. **KEY DATES: HIGHS 1–2; 28–29** A dynamic period when positive thinking can make a very real difference to your personal progress. **LOWS 15–16** A possible low point – focus on your personal life to try to make sense of things that have confused you recently.

AUGUST: MAIN TRENDS: 5–6 Trends bring you good insight into everyday problems and make this a good time for relating well with others. You may have a breakthrough in understanding a particular matter. **19–20** A breezy, taking-life-in-your stride approach works best now, especially if you encounter things that are new and unusual. **22–23** Some quick thinking at work could lead to progress. An excellent day to talk over plans and schemes. **KEY DATES: HIGHS 24–25** The opportunity for a change in your career could come from nowhere and see you gaining more freedom and leisure time. **LOWS 11–12** Right now it may seem nothing will go right. Keep your expectations low.

SEPTEMBER: MAIN TRENDS: 1–2 Don't be afraid to retreat from your everyday routine and seek comfort and inspiration from the past. Use your imagination, too. **22–23** You may now reap the benefit of some previous efforts, especially regarding your ambitions or money-making endeavours. **24–25** Take any opportunity to widen your horizons that comes along now and keep abreast of all current news and views in everyday life. **KEY DATES: HIGHS 20–21** Make the most of this time when Lady Luck is on your side! **LOWS 7–9** A feeling of uncertainty pervades your life, but you may have to make a decision nevertheless. Proceed cautiously.

OCTOBER: MAIN TRENDS: 14–15 Expanding matters at work may prove challenging and even expensive. Avoid taking major business or financial risks, and work within your limitations. **18–19** You may find the right kind of assistance arrives just when you need it – an eyebrow-raising proposal may come your way, and it could bring benefits for everyone around you. **23–24** A period of social success when you may see new, welcoming faces on the horizon. Business dealings should now go very much your way. **KEY DATES: HIGHS 18–19** Don't be afraid to act confidently and with courage to go for what you really want. **LOWS 4–6** Just for a short time, it may pay to know when you're really beaten. Thing will look up shortly.

NOVEMBER: MAIN TRENDS: 4–5 There's strength in numbers as others help raise your spirits. Make the most of personal meetings and conversations. **16–17** Focus on practical matters and clear up as many outstanding minor tasks as you can. **21–22** New casual contacts may not be appealing, and you may be much better off with familiar faces and places from the past. **KEY DATES: HIGHS 14–15** With the planets on your side, you can do little wrong now. **LOWS 1– 2; 29–30** If you feel something has put you right back at the start, let go of worry and consider your next option.

DECEMBER: MAIN TRENDS: 7–8 Your intuition and 'can do' attitude put you on the right path. A conversation with someone might make this all too clear. **14–15** You make an impact, and others want to please you. Use these trends to take some new control of your life. **20–21** Outings for pleasure and cultural interests are positively highlighted. An excellent time for a social gathering or a date. **KEY DATES: HIGHS 12–13** Don't be shy of hogging the limelight socially – you may impress new admirers! **LOWS 25–27** Prepare for some changes beyond your control and remember to expect the unexpected, Taurus.

GEMINI BORN PEOPLE
Birthdays: 22 May to 21 June inclusive
Planet: Mercury. Birthstone: Agate. Lucky day: Wednesday

Keynote for the Year: *A professional matter gains real momentum this year but will bring with it extra responsibilities. Trips into the past are significant and may bring much joy.*

JANUARY: MAIN TRENDS: 7–8 As the year begins, your chart reveals the power of travel so do all you can to widen your horizons. Cultural and mental interests could bring the same benefits if you can't get away. **23–24** Approach everything optimistically and you may fulfil your own prophecies. **26–27** Your imagination may be working overtime and you may struggle to focus. Confide in loved ones for reassurance if you need to. **KEY DATES: HIGHS 21–22** Trends favour your social life; look forward to something new. **LOWS 8–9** Events may be unpredictable, so take time to simply watch and wait.

FEBRUARY: MAIN TRENDS: 1–3 Trends suggest your love life will be generally uplifting and eventful – and you may get far more than you bargained for. **8–9** Use a little charm to help you achieve your personal ambitions or get the best from your partner. **19–20** Being at the forefront of the social action is really your forte today, and your talent for self-promotion should make getting your preferred reaction no trouble at all. **KEY DATES: HIGHS 17–18** A potentially lucky period and a great time for making fresh starts. **LOWS 4–6** Take one task at a time and avoid anything that seems more trouble than it's worth.

MARCH: MAIN TRENDS: 2–3 Your professional expectations are high, but you should be able to fulfil them. Others respond well to your attitude. **5–6** Trends suggest some financial improvement. An ideal time to commit yourself to new projects, especially in business partnerships. **20–21** If it arises, take the chance to widen your personal horizons and get what you can from life. Travel and study are especially favoured in your chart. **KEY DATES: HIGHS 15–16** You have enough energy to burn the candle at both ends. Trust your intuitive strengths. **LOWS 3–4; 30–31** We all need time to reflect; remember there's nothing wrong with slowing down a little.

APRIL: MAIN TRENDS: 2–3 This isn't the time to get stuck on certain ideas or carried away by emotion. You should be able to resolve a problem with your partner, but only if you play fairly. **20–21** Things move smoothly and productively at work, so much so that you feel your work itself is a joy. **22–23** The period of fulfilment through work and practical achievement continues. Enjoy this unplanned and unforced positive experience. **KEY DATES: HIGHS 12–13** Your talent for inspiring others may be an important factor now in your work. **LOWS 26–27** You may find it difficult to communicate properly – get on with something you can finish quickly and independently.

MAY: MAIN TRENDS: 2–3 Trends favour communications, so prepare to hear what seems to be exciting news. However, as always, check your facts carefully before you allow what you learn to lead you to make an impulsive move. **19–20** You may be at the front of the queue when it comes to saying your piece and be revelling in the attention but remember – the world doesn't revolve around you. **22–23** A social occasion could prove very stimulating as your communication with friends and colleagues flows smoothly and easily. **KEY DATES: HIGHS 9–10** Trends assist your powers of persuasion. **LOWS 23–25** Don't worry if you find life hard-going – take some rest.

JUNE: MAIN TRENDS: 3–4 You will thrive in an environment that allows you to think quietly and withdraw from the day-to-day hubbub. **24–25** You may feel the need to get on with things, especially at work, but avoid becoming impatient. **27–28** Expect the proverbial breath of fresh air and, perhaps, some opportunities to get ahead at work. You are optimistic and your goals are within reach.

KEY DATES: HIGHS 5–7 Trends suggest you may be moving up a few steps on the ladder of success. **LOWS 20–21** Try to keep life as simple and uncomplicated as possible.

JULY: MAIN TRENDS: 1–2 You may feel the urge to break out of mundane routine – and if you do so, you may meet some inspirational people. **10–11** Let yourself go and express yourself; even if you don't quite reach the audience you wanted, you'll benefit from your time in the spotlight. **22–23** Although you may be happy to see a job done well and are prepared to work hard, why not be more ambitious? **KEY DATES: HIGHS 3–4; 30–31** You will make a good leader at these times, and your success will boost your confidence. **LOWS 17–18** Prepare for a personal situation to run adrift, especially where practical matters are concerned.

AUGUST: MAIN TRENDS: 7–8 Current planetary influences reveal that money seems to be your main concern. Don't allow your worries to affect your friends and partners. **11–12** Get ready for whatever life sends your way – broaden your social horizons as there is someone, somewhere ready to assist you. **21–22** By talking openly, you may discover that someone's needs override yours today. Act rationally, whatever the situation. **KEY DATES: HIGHS 26–27** Lady Luck may assist your efforts at work. Capitalise on your good fortune. **LOWS 13–15** Keep to familiar faces and places if you want to get the best from life.

SEPTEMBER: MAIN TRENDS: 8–9 Your chart suggests that your best times will come through home and family right now. Go with the flow and enjoy it. **12–13** Set about tasks that need to be completed and do them your way. At work, this attitude may lead to opportunities for advancement. **28–29** Make some time for personal space and freedom; you may benefit from being on the move and open to new things. **KEY DATES: HIGHS 22–24** Under these trends, your judgement is good and problem solving is as easy as ABC. **LOWS 10–11** See this time as a chance to take a break from pressures and ambitions.

OCTOBER: MAIN TRENDS: 16–17 If you have financial matters to deal with, prepare for some delays and setbacks. You may need to be patient and take things slowly. **22–23** It's possible that you could find yourself at odds with others over a particular issue, but don't ignore their opinions – they may be proved to be right. **28–29** An excellent period career wise – your objectives should be easier to accomplish and your influence strengthens. **KEY DATES: HIGHS 20–21** If you can put your entire heart and soul into what you're doing now you may expect some big successes. **LOWS 7–8** You may lack staying power so look for fulfilment in simple things.

NOVEMBER: MAIN TRENDS: 4–5 If you're unsure about a recent decision, then leave it open-ended. Take time to rest and perhaps indulge yourself elsewhere. **11–12** If you see an opportunity to make a financial gain, make sure you don't leave outstanding projects unfinished while you pursue it. The influence of someone senior may be beneficial. **21–22** Let off steam by enjoying some social time. Also, you may learn something valuable from a friend. **KEY DATES: HIGHS 16–17** Trends bring you the boost of energy needed to assert yourself. **LOWS 3–4; 30** Take an easy-going attitude – a strict work schedule may see you defeated.

DECEMBER: MAIN TRENDS: 2–3 Your chart suggests that you may have to take stock of things and decide if there is something that's not working for you. If you choose to abandon something, be resolute in your decision. **7–8** The accent is on fun and leisure – you will be entertaining company for others and your creativity may be at a peak. **18–19** Look out for some assistance with a practical or financial plan, especially in the workplace. **KEY DATES: HIGHS 14–15** Give your full attention to a fresh start – it's a fruitful time for turning ideas into reality. **LOWS 1; 28–29** Avoid being introspective or spending too much time alone. Some light-hearted fun with someone close would be perfect.

Old Moore now Introduces you to Master Kuang and the Whispering Wisdom of your

CHINESE HOROSCOPE

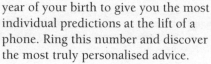

EVERY DAY – IF YOU LIKE

Let Old Moore introduce you to his friend **Kuang C. Wang**. He is the great Chinese Master, whom Old Moore has invited to join his *personalised daily advice service*. By allowing Master Kuang the use of his new and massive computer, Old Moore can provide you with new, top quality Chinese guidance and wisdom thinking.

There is here a motivational thought for you every day.

Your daily rendezvous with Old Moore's friend, Kuang C. Wang will cost but a few pence per day* and you can hear this authoritative guide to your life, work and happiness. This is not the usual 'fortune telling' patter, but enlightened insights into how best to exploit your potential on any given day.

Unlike any other astro phone service, Master Kuang will be working from the day, month and

year of your birth to give you the most individual predictions at the lift of a phone. Ring this number and discover the most truly personalised advice.

Down the centuries, successful Chinese people have used the benefits of their ancient wisdom systems. In their daily living, they draw upon a cocktail of positive guidance. They use Astrology, Feng Shui, I-Ching and carefully selected *whispering thoughts of wisdom* to guide them for each coming day.

Yes, every day, the Chinese system combines its elements to produce thoughts of *wisdom*, which can help you to get the best out of any day.

Today there is such a thought for you. Your Guiding Principle for the day. And you can carry it through the day to help your intuitive powers. They can so greatly improve your life. And the decisions you make during the day.

0906 880 5493

*Calls cost 60p per minute at all times
Charges may be higher for payphones and non-BT networks
Complaints & Service Provider (ATS): 0844 836 9769

2024 – Year of the Dragon

Chinese astrology works on a slightly different time scale from the more familiar Western branch of the study, and because of this Chinese New Year is marked on a different date each year. It is not, therefore, until 10 February in 2024 that the new year is celebrated, and the Year of the Dragon officially begins. At the beginning of 2024, the world is still under the rulership of the easy-going and affable Rabbit, and so a fairly settled time and a harmonious period can be expected.

Beyond 10 February, things start to become interesting. Dragon years are epitomized by activity and reaction. There is plenty of talking, but there is also a great deal happening and most of it leads to concrete results, even if the road is fraught with arguments and even a little danger. The Western zodiac sign associated with the Dragon is Aries, making this probably the most dynamic of all Chinese animal years, with no end of memorable, significant events.

The Element associated with the Dragon during 2024 is Wood. This brings a natural opposition to the fire-like quality of the Dragon and so it somewhat tones down the more reactive and potentially violent qualities of a Dragon year. As always during Dragon years, there are likely to be sudden flare-ups, which crackle and splutter like burning wood before settling down quite quickly. International situations will often seem more serious than they turn out to be, while accusations, scandals and revelations are highly likely. 'Never a dull moment' is the watchword.

In terms of global events, there is usually nothing settled about Dragon years. Things remain in a state of flux. No sooner has one world issue been sorted out, than another will start somewhere else, giving the impression at times that the whole planet is in a state of political and economic transition. Business could be extremely variable, but progress is likely to be made by those who really go for it and though stock markets will fluctuate wildly, the general trend is likely to be up.

Dragon years often see great scientific progress, and this is much amplified by the accompanying Wood element. Expect disasters on land, but also announcements about planting forests and the recreation of environments across the planet that have not been in evidence for thousands of years.

If you were born under the sign of the Dragon which, generally speaking, would mean your birthday fell in 1916, 1928, 1940, 1952, 1964, 1976, 1988, 2000 or 2012 you can expect 2024 to work very well for you. You will be firing on all cylinders, anxious to get moving and you will not easily be diverted from your plans.

Dragons are bold, adventurous, determined, strong and can endure great hardship. You may not have the best sense of humour in the world, especially if the joke's on you, but you know how to get things done. You can be noble, aspiring and good at resolving any problem or difficulty, whether caused by you or by others. In the main you stand for fairness, but you often choose to fight over debate, and there are times when you could achieve far more by simply talking things through.

CANCER BORN PEOPLE
Birthdays: 22 June to 22 July inclusive
Planet: Moon. Birthstone: Ruby. Lucky day: Monday

Keynote for the Year: *Expanding your social life should be no problem this year, but make sure to avoid narrow-mindedness or a tendency to see things only from your own perspective.*

JANUARY: MAIN TRENDS: 8–9 A career development may stall now if you neglect the finer details. Fortunately, family matters are more positively highlighted. **14–16** Your patience may be tested by loved ones who think they have your best interests at heart. But a certain degree of self-sacrifice may work wonders. **20–21** Trends enhance your social life and especially favour teamwork. Your powers of persuasion may stand you in good stead. **KEY DATES: HIGHS 23–24** Be open to new influences – they may lead to opportunities for success. **LOWS 10–11** Remain self-disciplined in the face of challenges.

FEBRUARY: MAIN TRENDS: 2–4 An emotionally rewarding time is indicated; you should find you get back what you put into partnerships, whether business or pleasure. **17–18** Your empathetic sensitivity to those around you should make you the perfect host. As someone opens up, you may also learn something. **22–23** Trends now make it difficult to move forward easily and compromise may be called for – delay any big decisions if you can. **KEY DATES: HIGHS 19–21** A great time to set a new idea in motion, the bigger, the better. **LOWS 7–8** Work may be demanding now; work hard but don't overstretch yourself.

MARCH: MAIN TRENDS: 1–2 A good time to concentrate on your work and to make improvements to your working practices. You may receive assistance or advice from others. **12–13** Trends suggest you will be popular now, and that you may make a dynamic impact on others, something that loved ones could find especially attractive. **20–22** Although you should prepare for some challenges at work you have what it takes to meet them head on and show others what you're made of. **KEY DATES: HIGHS 17–19** The beginning of an optimistic period when life could prove pretty exciting. **LOWS 5–6** Don't allow setbacks to scupper your plans; put them on the back burner while you ride out this temporary low patch.

APRIL: MAIN TRENDS: 3–4 Financially speaking, things tend to look brighter under this influence. Expect to enjoy life's pleasures more than usual. **12–13** Everything in life should be running smoothly, and you should have little difficulty in motivating others and attracting just the right sort of people. **21–22** Interesting talks and discussions should be enlivened by this influence – you have great insight into certain situations. **KEY DATES: HIGHS 14–15** With an optimistic outlook, you should achieve your goals with ease. This is also the ideal time to push yourself forward into new projects. **LOWS 1–2; 27–30** Play it safe if you must make an important decision and only go ahead with what you are sure will work.

MAY: MAIN TRENDS: 1–3 It could be time to move away from a situation, perhaps a personal relationship. Be aware of what isn't working out – but think carefully before you make any move. **9–10** A period for ringing the changes and embracing a broad-minded outlook. Trends suggest the chance for extended travel. **20–21** Whatever's most familiar tends to be most fulfilling now; family and friends are your best company as outside pressures slacken. **KEY DATES: HIGHS 11–12** Your chart suggests you could be lucky in something competitive now. **LOWS 26–27** You may have noticed a general lack of progress. Consider if you could make a sacrifice to get things moving again.

JUNE: MAIN TRENDS: 6–7 Life may make rather heavy demands on you – prepare to encounter obstacles or a personal disappointment. Keep a cool head. **12–14** Proper organisation is now a pre-requisite to short-term success – if you heed this, material rewards may be the result. **20–21** A rewarding period in social and romantic situations as you are more than willing to express yourself.

KEY DATES: HIGHS 8–9 For a while, anything may seem possible, and your optimistic attitude may help something go your way. **LOWS 22–23** Consider spending some quiet time alone to find a sense of inner contentment and fulfilment.

JULY: MAIN TRENDS: 10–11 With your strong views, you should avoid speaking in ways that might cause others to work against your interests. It's all a matter of presentation. **22–23** Your powers to influence others at work ought to be considerable as things take off and you are busy solving problems and moving things along. **26–27** Undaunted by a big responsibility, you should make a good job of your task, especially if you utilise your superior judgement. **KEY DATES: HIGHS 5–6** There may be something of the pioneer about you now; prepare for a good result if you project yourself strongly. **LOWS 19–20** Don't expect too much of yourself and take an easy-going approach if something is unclear.

AUGUST: MAIN TRENDS: 4–5 Beware of a disagreement if you need to co-operate with someone on a certain matter. You may find it hard to get your message across. **18–19** You are not lacking in the inner strength and optimism needed to succeed – you may even receive an unexpected helping hand. **23–24** Trends highlight communication in your chart – you'll be quick off the mark and have what it takes to get your ideas heard. **KEY DATES: HIGHS 1–2; 28–30** This trend brings out all your best qualities and could be your luckiest time. **LOWS 16–17** Don't push yourself, or strain too much, and you should be contented.

SEPTEMBER: MAIN TRENDS: 4–5 Friends are supportive and loved ones are more likely to reach out to you now – you may benefit from a new acquaintance. **10–11** A favourable time to be socially active. Your charming, upbeat outlook enhances your attractiveness. **22–23** Domestically, a period of fulfilment when there may be nostalgia in the air – perhaps an encounter with an old familiar face. **KEY DATES: HIGHS 25–27** Lady Luck may enhance your personal influence over everyday matters. **LOWS 12–13** Take a slow and methodical approach to the business of the day – there are potential pitfalls ahead.

OCTOBER: MAIN TRENDS: 6–7 Trends suggest that certain projects could be winding up at work, but you should have new ideas up your sleeve. **18–19** Some social highlights are indicated – go all out to broaden your horizons as meetings and encounters may inspire some new ideas today. **25–26** Practical matters should prove easy enough as your competitive drive, initiative and physical energy are intensified. **KEY DATES: HIGHS 22–23** The monthly high sees you determined to pave your own way towards your goals. **LOWS 9–11** Hang fire on your plans temporarily or they may be inclined to go awry.

NOVEMBER: MAIN TRENDS: 1–2 So many interesting things appear to be happening now and your mind is quick and sharp, although your mood may be somewhat mercurial. **8–9** Day to day events move briskly, so much so that you may be hard-pressed to keep up with them. Travel arrangements may have to be re-scheduled. **22–23** You won't feel like taking on the rest of the world now – this is a time best reserved for private contemplation and minimising contact with others. **KEY DATES: HIGHS 18–20** A progressive phase; something you left on the shelf a while ago can now be dusted down and revitalised. **LOWS 6–7** Major decisions are best left alone while this planetary low is in operation.

DECEMBER: MAIN TRENDS: 1–2 You should make a good impression on others, especially someone senior at work. People really like you now. **5–6** Your chart indicates good communication with those closest to you; confiding in them could prove beneficial as you may learn something significant. **21–22** Push your personal boundaries and enjoy freedom through travel. But take along a companion for the ride. **KEY DATES: HIGHS 16–17** Financial matters should improve, whether through job-seeking or investments, as your approach is both intuitive and realistic. **LOWS 3–4** You may be lacking in confidence during this low patch so keep your expectations simple.

LEO BORN PEOPLE
Birthdays: 23 July to 23 August inclusive
Planet: Sun. Birthstone: Sapphire. Lucky day: Sunday

Keynote for the Year: *If emotional relationships are to succeed this year, they may require extra give and take. There are gains to be had in your career aspirations.*

JANUARY: MAIN TRENDS: 7–8 A certain lack of focus and persistence in the professional sphere may mean you're expecting results too soon, especially if you're working alone. Be patient. **19–20** How you use new information is vital – now is the time to initiate plans you've had up your sleeve and enlist others to assist you. **28–29** There is a warmheartedness in you which makes you very attractive to others. You may even attract a new love interest. **KEY DATES: HIGHS 25–27** Maintain a high profile and you should successfully broaden your professional contacts. **LOWS 12–13** Your judgement could be affected by this planetary influence; suspend major decisions until this period has passed.

FEBRUARY: MAIN TRENDS: 1–2 Career wise, whatever you're doing now has the potential for success. Don't be afraid to take action to turn your desires into reality. **17–18** Trends highlight close personal relationships and companionship – you should be popular with others and be able to fit into all situations. **20– 21** Right now you are focused on family life. Here's where real fulfilment lies, although renovations may be needed at home. **KEY DATES: HIGHS 22–23** Your plans should run pretty much as expected. A small, measured risk may be advantageous. **LOWS 9–10** Take some time to consider the reality of your situation.

MARCH: MAIN TRENDS: 5–6 A crucial matter is now coming to a head; trends suggest that you'll soon be able to seize the initiative and move things in a different direction. **12–13** Analyse a current personal issue as you may need to jettison some of your own baggage. In simple terms, eliminate the unnecessary. **22–23** It may be necessary to say and do the right thing with a certain person. This shouldn't be difficult once you have summoned your courage. **KEY DATES: HIGHS 20–21** A long-past action may lead to an unexpected bonus! **LOWS 7–8** Prepare for some irritation if you must handle a heavy responsibility. Try to remain objective and keep things simple if possible.

APRIL: MAIN TRENDS: 6–7 Trends assist your efforts to get on the right side of people, especially at work. **8–9** There are times when a situation calls for a quick decision. Your chart suggests that it's now time to make your mind up about a significant matter. **21–22** Your relationship with your close partner should be rewarding; don't be afraid to bring powerful emotions to the surface and express yourself. **KEY DATES: HIGHS 16–18** The monthly high brings you powerful self-expression and confidence; use these to take advantage of all opportunities, especially financial. **LOWS 3–4** If life is testing you, see it as a challenge!

MAY: MAIN TRENDS: 9–10 You are reflective, warm-hearted and nostalgic under this trend. Your family life should be very rewarding. **20–21** Prepare to face some rather challenging personal situations. Don't allow anyone to undermine your sense of security. **22–23** Work and all practical matters are highlighted in your chart – this could mean important matters to deal with in the workplace, or perhaps just being busy at home. **KEY DATES: HIGHS 13–15** A plan brought to fruition now may be successful; in fact, many things are possible under this beneficial influence. **LOWS 1–2; 28–29** If there is a disagreement in a personal matter, break the deadlock and reach a resolution.

JUNE: MAIN TRENDS: 1–3 The beginning of an exciting period in your social and love life; get out and enjoy some fun. **18–19** Your strength lies in your ability to empathise; someone close may find your words reassuringly wise. **22–23** The mood lightens in your personal life; make the most of this and use your charm to put yourself in the spotlight and get things going your way. **KEY DATES: HIGHS 10–11** There may be more than one way of making progress – go for it. **LOWS 24–25** Put any major projects on the backburner and get on with something simple that can be completed easily.

JULY: MAIN TRENDS: 3–4 A challenging phase is indicated, as new ideas coming from others require your undivided attention. But will you be listening to them? **12–13** The time is right to pursue certain practical objectives, though you may have to put in extra hours. Professionally, you may achieve success over a competitor. **24–25** You are attractive to others and surrounded by good company. You may also benefit from your money-making talents. **KEY DATES: HIGHS 7–9** Prepare for some great opportunities to emerge, and to successfully achieve your objectives during this positive phase. **LOWS 21–23** Don't get carried away with your own big ideas; consider the feelings of those around you.

AUGUST: MAIN TRENDS: 6–8 Focus on your finances and how you might capitalise on any recent achievements. Planetary changes suggest this is a good time to sell your ideas or make agreements. **21–22** Insightful and intuitive, this is an intellectual peak. Some interesting communication with colleagues is indicated. **23–25** Your private life may come under scrutiny – be as open as possible where your feelings are concerned. **KEY DATES: HIGHS 3–5; 31** Some good results are in the offing, especially at work. **LOWS 18–19** Your ability to deal with something frustrating may tell you much about yourself.

SEPTEMBER: MAIN TRENDS: 1–2 In a good and confident mood, this is the time to show some personal leadership and play to your strengths. **22–23** You may feel the need for the stimulation of travel and contact with interesting people to keep you occupied. A good time for information gathering and initiating ideas. **24–25** Don't be afraid to ask for help – the planets strengthen your emotional ties and someone close should now offer you a shoulder to lean on. **KEY DATES: HIGHS 1; 27–28** Your ambitions rise to the surface and may lead you to consider big life changes. **LOWS 14–15** Keep your ego in check during this emotionally volatile period.

OCTOBER: MAIN TRENDS: 4–5 Trends suggest that some of the finer things of life may find their way to you through the help of loved one. **18–19** A social group or organisation with which you are involved may offer you new opportunities, perhaps even in a business sense. **24–25** Expect to need some will power at work today but avoid any tendency to act impulsively. **KEY DATES: HIGHS 24–26** You may have new and promising ideas in work or business – put them into operation. **LOWS 12–13** Bear in mind that this may not be the luckiest time for you, so work alone, if you can, to clear up unfinished business.

NOVEMBER: MAIN TRENDS: 12–13 You understand the value of a positive mental attitude and the need for empathy in all your dealings. Courage and confidence are on the increase. **16–17** Trends highlight meetings, discussions and appointments – your wonderful capacity for looking on the bright side may mean you are inspirational to others. **24–25** Expect a pleasant and co-operative atmosphere in personal relationships. You may now have the opportunity to show off a little in any area of life! **KEY DATES: HIGHS 21–22** Make an early start if you have a practical matter to complete. You may be laying the groundwork for future success. **LOWS 8–9** Avoid being careless or taking unnecessary risks which could result in setbacks.

DECEMBER: MAIN TRENDS: 7–8 Your chart reveals a new opening in your career – keep an open mind to the opportunities around you. **12–14** Seek independence, and a break from the norm – you will enjoy getting away from routines and doing something different. **21–22** Your ego receives a boost; make the most of it with social or group gatherings. **KEY DATES: HIGHS 18–19** If you get the chance to do your own thing, take it. **LOWS 5–6** The low makes you a little vulnerable – avoid anything that sounds too good to be true.

VIRGO BORN PEOPLE

Birthdays: 24 August to 23 September inclusive
Planet: Mercury. Birthstone: Sardonyx. Lucky day: Wednesday

Keynote for the Year: *One of your best years for travel or for taking up new spiritual pursuits; personal relationships, on the other hand, may require a common-sense and realistic approach.*

JANUARY: MAIN TRENDS: 12–13 As trends enhance your communication skills, conversations with those close to you should be warm and affectionate. **23–24** You will go far to avoid any confrontation, but don't simply hope that setbacks will disappear if you ignore them – they won't! **24–26** Broaden your mind and seek some intellectual or perhaps cultural inspiration. You will work well in a partnership – be on the lookout for new faces. **KEY DATES: HIGHS 1–2; 28–29** Trends indicate a favourable new start in any area. **LOWS 14–15** Prepare for a let-down in a personal matter and for things to not go quite your way.

FEBRUARY: MAIN TRENDS: 8–10 You may have the chance to change in your life in some way connected with things outside the home, possibly including some extended travel. Good strategy is now of the utmost importance. **22–23** Explore your creative side – you feel the need to impress someone now, so it might as well be yourself! Your social and romantic life is on the up. **28–29** In the world of money-making, use bold, innovative ideas to build secure foundations, especially if you are job seeking. **KEY DATES: HIGHS 24–26** The monthly high gives you a boost along the road to success. **LOWS 11–12** Avoid relying on instinct and instead research things thoroughly.

MARCH: MAIN TRENDS: 7–8 You may have to overcome an initial sense of inertia at work, but this won't prevent you making the most of the current progressive planetary influences. **17–18** A trend which may facilitate tricky problem solving, whether in practical or emotional issues. A loved one may be the source of some vital information. **30–31** Develop your understanding of life through contact with new friends now. A great time for travel and new environments. **KEY DATES: HIGHS 22–24** Effective action in the outside world may see your material goals come together very nicely. **LOWS 9–10** Play it safe during this temporary low phase.

APRIL: MAIN TRENDS: 2–3 If someone is over-assertive, either meet them on their own level or keep away. **21–22** Loved ones should be very reassuring, helping you to feel amiable and warm. In other areas, don't dither over a decision. **26–27** Casual interactions should be harmonious, which suits you as you may prefer to avoid some of life's harder realities. Short trips should be rewarding. **KEY DATES: HIGHS 19–20** You should find it easy to get your own way and may enjoy taking a chance, especially if you feel lucky! **LOWS 5–6** Beware a feeling of invincibility now – it's because you're taking on more than you can handle.

MAY: MAIN TRENDS: 19–20 A time of personal renewal when certain issues may come to an end, and you may find it useful to review and bring your plans up to date. **23–24** Keep yourself busy and enjoy your hobbies and pastimes, some of which may be unusual. You should be able to handle changes with ease. **28–29** Try to project yourself with originality – you may inspire others with your ability to set yourself apart and maximise your own innate talents. **KEY DATES: HIGHS 16–17** Approach any task you're engaged in with practicality and realism. **LOWS 3–4; 30–31** Prepare to have to work hard and to accept some limitations.

JUNE: MAIN TRENDS: 7–8 An excellent time to take up new studies, intellectual interests or anything that expands your mental horizons. **15–16** Developing personal interactive skills should be your main aim right now – you are at your happiest (and best) when things function smoothly. **21–23** Trends now favour your career – get yourself organised at work to avoid some standard pitfalls and you should be successful. **KEY DATES: HIGHS 12–14** A brand new scheme should be well underway and properly on target. **LOWS 26–27** A time of falling energy when you may feel discouraged. Bear in mind that this won't last long.

JULY: MAIN TRENDS: 1–3 Work and money matters are positively highlighted now, and it may well be that you find it easy to get what you want from life. **22–23** There are matters you should keep close to your chest, and a financial one may need a very cautious approach. **26–27** A good time to reassess your attachment to certain possessions or even people. Are they good for you or are you just trying to hang on to them? **KEY DATES: HIGHS 10–11** Trends suggest you may hear good news about a plan of action – if you feel confident enough, test your luck a little. **LOWS 24–25** Take time to recharge your batteries while the Moon is in your opposite sign.

AUGUST: MAIN TRENDS: 1–2 Don't let anything interfere with the normal flow of business and keep certain plans under wraps until you are certain of success. **17–18** A period of regeneration, when you realise that life could be much simpler if you offload unnecessary baggage. **23–24** Think twice before you make any major decisions, and make sure people do not misunderstand your intentions. **KEY DATES: HIGHS 6–7** Personal objectives take a turn for the better and you may get the chance to capitalise on fresh ideas. **LOWS 20–21** This trend may see a dwindling of energy – perhaps you need time to rest and revive yourself.

SEPTEMBER: MAIN TRENDS: 8–9 Prepare for a feelgood factor in personal relationships, and for meetings with business associates to also go well. **10–11** Use your analytical skills to think things through properly and make choices. Information gathering is also positively highlighted. **14–15** Not a big social time, as you are inclined to focus on everything most personal and private about yourself. Get down to basics and rid yourself of unnecessary accoutrements. **KEY DATES: HIGHS 2–4; 29–30** A 'green light' period in all areas of life – get an early start to make the most of it. **LOWS 16–17** Don't be anxious if the pace of progress naturally stalls a little now.

OCTOBER: MAIN TRENDS: 3–4 You feel the need to break free of restrictions at work. The foundations on which you build your life are now being tested, even if only in a minor way. **21–22** Trends bring a boost to professional matters, so focus on your career. Can you bring something to a successful conclusion? **29–31** Prepare to receive recognition for your achievements. Don't be shy of demonstrating your personal leadership skills. **KEY DATES: HIGHS 1; 27–28** Favourable planetary influences make short-term plans easier to realise. **LOWS 14–15** An unlucky time to make a vital decision – delay it until your energy and focus returns.

NOVEMBER. MAIN TRENDS: 8–9 You're best off on your own now; enjoy your independence and autonomy. **10–11** Trends help you to see that you don't need to struggle; anything that is winding down is doing so because it's the right time. **21–22** Take any opportunity to communicate your personal ideas with authority. You are pleasant company for most people, now. **KEY DATES: HIGHS 23–24** A good time to begin something new, as trends make you energetic and competitive and bring you vitality and self-confidence. **LOW 10–11** Try to be adaptable if something is no longer working for you.

DECEMBER: MAIN TRENDS: 1–2 Emotional matters may be on the agenda and the sooner you talk them over with a trusted confidante, the better. **14–15** Your active phase slows down and you take things at a more leisurely pace. Prepare to be plagued by a domestic intrusion of some kind. **24–25** Social invitations come thick and fast this Christmas – choose whatever brings you most pleasure.. **KEY DATES: HIGHS 20–22** With a great deal of self-confidence, you now have what it takes to find new solutions to old problems. **LOWS 7–9** Don't be over-concerned with achievement – this is a time to lie low and recuperate.

The UK's Leading Psychic Service
Voted No.1 by Customers

Visit Us Online :: www.Trusted-Psychics.co.uk

One of the highest respected psychic services bringing hope and comfort to thousands of callers across the world. Our handpicked readers are passionate about their work, to offer you future clarity, whatever your circumstances.

What We Can Offer You

★ Love Questions Answered In Clear Expert Detail
★ Work / Career / Money / Finance Readings
★ Unique Horoscope / Astrology Predictions
★ Family / Friends Detailed Readings Online
★ Mediumship / Personal Spirit Messages
★ Clairvoyant Specialist Readings Online
★ Personal Clear Future Life Predictions
★ Incredible Handpicked Tarot Readers

NO.1 PSYCHIC TEAM

Start Your Personal Reading Today

 Call Us Today 0906 360 7385

 Credit Card VISA 🔴 01604 922761

 Text Your Questions 07441 908 897

Cheapest Psychic Readings

Call our dedicated team of experienced Psychics, Mediums, Clairvoyants, Fortune Tellers and Tarot readers commited in offering clear guidance about your life's future path. **Excellence is our only standard.**

★★★★★ Love & Relationship Experts

Love Specialists

Clairvoyants

Mediumship

Service by LiveLines UK Ltd. Calls cost 65p plus network access charges apply. We send promo msgs, call Helpline 03332002321 to opt out. Calls recorded. 18+ only. PO6538 NN2 7YN. Payments@livelinesuk.com.

JANUARY

For High Water add 5h 30m for Bristol, 4h 23m for Hull, 0h 43m for Leith; subtract 2h 21m for Dublin, 1h 26m for Greenock, 2h 29m for Liverpool.

D of M	D of W	Festivals, Events and Anniversaries	Sun at London Rises	Sun at London Sets	High Water at London Bridge am	High Water at London Bridge pm	Moon at London Rises	Moon at London Sets	Weather
			h m	h m	h m	h m	h m	h m	
1	M	New Year's Day	08:06	16:01	04:37	17:06	21:52	11:06	
2	Tu	Bank holiday (Scotland)	08:06	16:02	05:09	17:41	23:02	11:17	
3	W	Luther excommunicated 1521	08:05	16:03	05:43	18:20	—	11:26	
4	Th	Fay Weldon d. 2023	08:05	16:04	06:21	19:03	00:11	11:36	
5	F	Bradley Cooper b. 1975	08:05	16:06	07:07	19:58	01:23	11:48	
6	Sa	Epiphany	08:05	16:07	08:07	21:06	02:38	12:02	
7	Su	Tower of Pisa closes 1990	08:04	16:08	09:35	22:13	03:57	12:20	
8	M	ANC founded 1912	08:04	16:09	10:46	23:17	05:19	12:47	
9	Tu	Princess of Wales b. 1982	08:03	16:11	11:47	—	06:40	13:27	
10	W	Treaty of Versailles 1920	08:03	16:12	00:18	12:44	07:50	14:26	
11	Th	Earl of Essex exec. 1591	08:02	16:14	01:12	13:37	08:44	15:45	
12	F	Lisa-Marie Presley d. 2023	08:02	16:15	02:02	14:27	09:22	17:16	
13	Sa	Michael Bond b. 1926	08:01	16:16	02:48	15:15	09:48	18:50	
14	Su	First Gallup poll 1937	08:00	16:18	03:33	16:02	10:06	20:22	
15	M	Wikipedia goes on-line 2001	07:59	16:20	04:16	16:48	10:21	21:50	
16	Tu	Shackleton at S. Pole 1909	07:59	16:21	04:58	17:35	10:34	23:15	
17	W	Anne Bronte b. 1820	07:58	16:23	05:41	18:24	10:47	—	
18	Th	Rudyard Kipling d. 1936	07:57	16:24	06:27	19:18	11:00	00:39	
19	F	Feast of St Wulfstan	07:56	16:26	07:24	20:16	11:17	02:03	
20	Sa	D'hess of Edinburgh b. 1965	07:55	16:28	08:33	21:20	11:38	03:27	
21	Su	Mosley rally 1934	07:54	16:29	09:46	22:30	12:07	04:48	
22	M	Ramsay MacDonald PM 1924	07:52	16:31	11:00	23:42	12:47	06:01	
23	Tu	Salvador Dali d. 1989	07:51	16:33	—	12:08	13:40	07:02	
24	W	Gold discovered, CA, 1848	07:50	16:34	00:41	13:04	14:46	07:48	
25	Th	Burns Night	07:49	16:36	01:29	13:51	15:59	08:20	
26	F	Australia Day	07:48	16:38	02:09	14:32	17:14	08:43	
27	Sa	Holocaust Memorial Day	07:46	16:40	02:45	15:08	18:27	09:00	
28	Su	Hutton Inquiry published 2004	07:45	16:41	03:16	15:41	19:39	09:13	
29	M	Anton Chekhov b. 1869	07:44	16:43	03:46	16:10	20:49	09:24	
30	Tu	Geraldine McEwan d. 2015	07:42	16:45	04:16	16:40	21:58	09:33	
31	W	Corn Laws abolished 1849	07:41	16:47	04:46	17:11	23:08	09:43	

Following a cold start, extensive snowfall in the north and east early in the month. A more usual rainy pattern follows, with a boisterous wind from north-west to south-east.

MOON'S PHASES JANUARY 2024			Days	Hours	Mins
	☾	Last Quarter	4	03	30
	●	New Moon	11	11	57
	☽	First Quarter	18	03	52
	○	Full Moon	25	17	54

All times on this page are GMT

PREDICTIONS

The New Moon on 11 January falls in Capricorn on the Midheaven, in an opposition to the United Kingdom Moon and a trine to Uranus. There is a high prospect of constitutional change in the UK, with proposals for new relationships between England, Wales, Scotland and Northern Ireland, and changes to the voting system. We may see imminent reforms to property taxes and investment regulations. All political parties will emphasise the need to rebuild institutions and essential infrastructure. Planetary pressures focus on southern Africa, with great power rivalry prompting investment opportunities, however civil insurrection is likely to break out as old political affiliations resurface.

The Full Moon on 25 January falls in Leo in the twelfth house at London and Jupiter is on the Midheaven. The mood is one of optimism and hope, and a sense that economic conditions are improving could lead to increased spending but also higher inflation. Health issues top the agenda, including mental health and sexually transmitted diseases. The welfare of children is a focus for legislators. We may expect a scandal concerning spies or subversion in Whitehall. Central America enters a short-term unstable phase but offers generally good returns for new speculators.

At the Warwick *Classic Handicap Chase*, a 10-year-old carrying 10st 4lb may triumph.

FEBRUARY

For High Water add 5h 30m for Bristol, 4h 23m for Hull, 0h 43m for Leith; subtract 2h 21m for Dublin, 1h 26m for Greenock, 2h 29m for Liverpool.

D of M	D of W	Festivals, Events and Anniversaries	Sun at London Rises	Sun at London Sets	High Water at London Bridge am	High Water at London Bridge pm	Moon at London Rises	Moon at London Sets	Weather
			h m	h m	h m	h m	h m	h m	
1	Th	Mary Shelley d. 1851	07:39	16:48	05:16	17:44	—	09:53	A month in two distinct sections as at first snow returns in the north with accompanying north wind in most parts; then milder, wet and sunny periods to follow.
2	F	Candlemas Day	07:38	16:50	05:48	18:20	00:20	10:06	
3	Sa	Tim Flowers b. 1967	07:36	16:52	06:27	19:03	01:36	10:21	
4	Su	Washington US Pres. 1789	07:34	16:54	07:15	19:59	02:55	10:43	
5	M	Regency period beg. 1811	07:33	16:56	08:22	21:18	04:15	11:15	
6	Tu	Access. Elizabeth II 1952	07:31	16:58	10:02	22:41	05:29	12:04	
7	W	Grenada independent 1974	07:29	16:59	11:20	12:54	06:31	13:12	
8	Th	Burt Bacharach d. 2023	07:28	17:01	—	12:26	07:16	14:38	
9	F	Princess Margaret d. 2002	07:26	17:03	00:55	13:23	07:47	16:13	
10	Sa	Chinese New Year (Dragon)	07:24	17:05	01:47	14:14	08:09	17:49	
11	Su	Henry VIII head of CoE 1534	07:22	17:07	02:33	15:02	08:25	19:22	
12	M	*Bagpuss* begins 1974	07:21	17:09	03:17	15:47	08:39	20:52	
13	Tu	Shrove Tuesday	07:19	17:10	03:58	16:30	08:52	22:20	
14	W	Ash Wed/St Valentine	07:17	17:12	04:39	17:13	09:06	23:47	
15	Th	Graham Hill b. 1929	07:15	17:14	05:19	17:57	09:21	—	
16	F	Southampton a city 1964	07:13	17:16	06:02	18:43	09:41	01:14	
17	Sa	Patricia Routledge b. 1929	07:11	17:18	06:52	19:35	10:07	02:38	
18	Su	First Sunday in Lent	07:09	17:20	07:56	20:37	10:44	03:54	
19	M	Merle Oberon b. 1911	07:07	17:21	09:14	21:56	11:34	04:59	
20	Tu	Feast of St Basil	07:05	17:23	10:38	23:21	12:36	05:49	
21	W	Margot Fonteyn d. 1991	07:03	17:25	11:55	—	13:47	06:24	
22	Th	Robert II Scottish king 1371	07:01	17:27	00:23	12:52	15:01	06:49	
23	F	Fangio kidnapped 1958	06:59	17:29	01:11	13:37	16:15	07:07	
24	Sa	Russia invades Ukraine 2022	06:57	17:30	01:51	14:15	17:27	07:21	
25	Su	Sir Don Bradman d. 2001	06:55	17:32	02:25	14:48	18:38	07:32	
26	M	World Trade Ctr bomb 1993	06:53	17:34	02:55	15:17	19:47	07:42	
27	Tu	Betty Boothroyd d. 2023	06:51	17:36	03:22	15:44	20:57	07:51	
28	W	UK hung parliament 1974	06:49	17:38	03:51	16:11	22:08	08:01	
29	Th	Agadir earthquake 1960	06:46	17:39	04:20	16:40	23:22	08:12	

MOON'S PHASES FEBRUARY 2024			Days	Hours	Mins
	☾	Last Quarter	2	23	18
	●	New Moon	9	22	59
	☽	First Quarter	16	15	00
	○	Full Moon	24	12	30

All times on this page are GMT

PREDICTIONS

The New Moon on 9 February falls in Aquarius in the fourth house in London and a square to Uranus. The dominant mood worldwide will be excitable, revolutionary and unstable. In the UK, economic optimism will be challenged by unexpected events, such as a major bankruptcy. Financial regulators may have to step in with instant solutions. However, the property market is essentially stable and investments in innovative technology remain a strong option. Scotland enters a major change of transition, reconsidering its long-term future. Russia enters a phase of maximum internal stress, with dissent breaking out in the regions.

The Full Moon on 24 February falls in Virgo. The Sun is in a conjunction with Saturn on the Midheaven at London; Pluto, Venus and Mars are in a conjunction in the eighth house. In the UK, the government will promote a grand vision of the country's future, but the best initiatives will collapse amid incompetence and confusion. There may be election fever and arguments about how long the government can last. Northern Ireland enters a phase of reorganisation, with communities coming together to reach a new long-term political consensus. China enters a two-year period of intense constitutional and democratic challenge.

A horse carrying 10st 9lb may be victor at Newbury's Betfair *Hurdle*, while an 11-year-old may win in the Betfair *Ascot Chase*.

European Army ?

MARCH

For High Water add 5h 30m for Bristol, 4h 23m for Hull, 0h 43m for Leith; subtract 2h 21m for Dublin, 1h 26m for Greenock, 2h 29m for Liverpool.

D of M	D of W	Festivals, Events and Anniversaries	Sun at London Rises	Sun at London Sets	High Water at London Bridge am	High Water at London Bridge pm	Moon at London Rises	Moon at London Sets	Weather
			h m	h m	h m	h m	h m	h m	
1	F	St David's Day	06:44	17:41	04:49	17:11	—	08:28	
2	Sa	Mikhail Gorbachev b. 1931	06:42	17:43	05:21	17:45	00:38	08:45	
3	Su	Jean Harlow b. 1911	06:40	17:45	05:57	18:25	01:57	09:11	
4	M	Kenny Dalglish b. 1951	06:38	17:46	06:44	19:16	03:12	09:51	
5	Tu	Henry VI deposed 1461	06:36	17:48	07:47	20:29	04:18	10:48	
6	W	George Formby d. 1961	06:33	17:50	09:28	22:09	05:09	12:04	
7	Th	Bonaparte captures Jaffa 1799	06:31	17:52	10:57	23:31	05:45	13:33	
8	F	Int. Women's Day	06:29	17:53	—	12:08	06:10	15:08	
9	Sa	Mystic Meg d. 2023	06:27	17:55	00:35	13:06	06:29	16:43	
10	Su	Mother's Day/Ramadan beg.	06:24	17:57	01:26	13:56	06:44	18:16	
11	M	Commonwealth Day	06:22	17:58	02:11	14:42	06:57	19:48	
12	Tu	Moscow Russia capital 1918	06:20	18:00	02:54	15:25	07:10	21:19	
13	W	Uranus discovered 1781	06:18	18:02	03:35	16:06	07:25	22:49	
14	Th	Karl Marx d. 1883	06:15	18:04	04:16	16:47	07:43	—	
15	F	Andrew Jackson b. 1767	06:13	18:05	04:56	17:27	08:07	00:18	
16	Sa	Feast of St Julian	06:11	18:07	05:39	18:08	08:41	01:41	
17	Su	St Patrick's Day	06:09	18:09	06:27	18:55	09:27	02:53	
18	M	Grover Cleveland b. 1837	06:06	18:10	07:27	19:55	10:26	03:48	
19	Tu	Alka-Seltzer on sale 1931	06:04	18:12	08:45	21:18	11:35	04:28	
20	W	Spring equinox 03 06	06:02	18:14	10:11	22:49	12:49	04:55	
21	Th	Pocahontas d. 1617	06:00	18:16	11:31	23:55	14:03	05:15	
22	F	William Shatner b. 1931	05:57	18:17	—	12:28	15:16	05:30	
23	Sa	UK Covid lockdown 2020	05:55	18:19	00:43	13:11	16:27	05:41	
24	Su	Palm Sunday	05:53	18:21	01:22	13:48	17:37	05:51	
25	M	Holi/Lunar eclipse 04 53	05:50	18:22	01:56	14:19	18:46	06:01	
26	Tu	Driving test introduced 1934	05:48	18:24	02:27	14:47	19:57	06:10	
27	W	Arnold Bennett d. 1931	05:46	18:26	02:55	15:13	21:11	06:21	
28	Th	Maundy Thursday	05:44	18:27	03:23	15:41	22:27	06:34	
29	F	Good Friday	05:41	18:29	03:54	16:12	23:44	06:50	
30	Sa	Queen Mother d. 2002	05:39	18:31	04:26	16:44	—	07:13	
31	Su	Easter Sunday	05:37	18:32	05:00	17:18	01:01	07:47	

Weather column note (vertical): A flourishing early spring will feature mild, mostly dry weather throughout. Often sunny and settled, with an especially early spring bloom in the south of the UK

MOON'S PHASES MARCH 2024

			Days	Hours	Mins
☾	Last Quarter		3	15	23
●	New Moon		10	09	00
☽	First Quarter		17	04	10
○	Full Moon		25	07	00

All times on this page are GMT (Add 1 hr BST from 27th)

PREDICTIONS

The New Moon on 10 March falls in Pisces in a conjunction with Saturn and Neptune in the eleventh cusp at London. Jupiter and Uranus are conjunct in the twelfth house. There is a move towards greater idealism in politics and a shift to the Left and to compassionate socialism. The medical area offers especially strong investment profits. There is an ongoing concern over subversion and threats to democracy. Investment in advanced communications and biomedical technology is indicated and we could see technological breakthroughs. The control and organisation of the oceans and water resources will be significant.

The Full Moon on 25 March is a lunar eclipse in Libra. Saturn and Venus are in a conjunction in Pisces, and Jupiter and Uranus are in a conjunction in Taurus. Mental and physical health concerns take centre stage, along with problems related to food production, pollution of farmland and diet. There is a recognition that individual health is linked to wider social and environmental concerns. In Scotland, the political system is afflicted by confusion and is on the verge of meltdown. EU countries take steps towards increased military cooperation. High internal tension continues in Russia.

The Cheltenham *Gold Cup* may be won by an 8-year-old outsider, whilst Sandown's *Imperial Cup Handicap Hurdle* could be taken by a 7-year-old carrying 10st 8lb.

Confrontation

APRIL

For High Water add 5h 30m for Bristol, 4h 23m for Hull, 0h 43m for Leith; subtract 2h 21m for Dublin, 1h 26m for Greenock, 2h 29m for Liverpool.

D of M	D of W	Festivals, Events and Anniversaries	Sun at London Rises	Sun at London Sets	High Water at London Bridge am	High Water at London Bridge pm	Moon at London Rises	Moon at London Sets	Weather
			h m	h m	h m	h m	h m	h m	
1	M	Easter Monday	05:34	18:34	05:38	17:58	02:09	08:36	
2	Tu	Battle of Copenhagen 1801	05:32	18:36	06:27	18:50	03:04	09:43	
3	W	Nigel Lawson d. 2023	05:30	18:37	07:32	20:02	03:44	11:05	
4	Th	Finland join NATO 2023	05:28	18:39	09:10	21:43	04:12	12:35	
5	F	*Mayflower* sails home 1621	05:25	18:41	10:36	23:05	04:32	14:07	
6	Sa	Raphael d. 1520	05:23	18:42	11:46	—	04:48	15:39	
7	Su	Low Sunday	05:21	18:44	00:09	12:44	05:02	17:10	
8	M	Solar eclipse 15 42/Eid	05:19	18:46	01:00	13:33	05:15	18:42	
9	Tu	Eid-al Fitr	05:17	18:47	01:46	14:18	05:29	20:14	
10	W	New York Tribune pub. 1841	05:14	18:49	02:29	15:00	05:45	21:46	
11	Th	Apollo 13 launched 1970	05:12	18:51	03:11	15:40	06:06	23:16	
12	F	Brexit Party launch 2019	05:10	18:52	03:52	16:20	06:36	—	
13	Sa	Amritsar massacre 1919	05:08	18:54	04:35	16:59	07:17	00:36	
14	Su	Highway Code issued 1931	05:06	18:56	05:18	17:38	08:13	01:40	
15	M	*Titanic* sinks 1912	05:03	18:57	06:06	18:22	09:21	02:27	
16	Tu	Sir Peter Ustinov b. 1921	05:01	18:59	07:03	19:18	10:35	02:59	
17	W	Benjamin Franklin b. 1790	04:59	19:01	08:16	20:38	11:50	03:21	
18	Th	Zimbabwe named 1980	04:57	19:02	09:33	22:02	13:04	03:38	
19	F	Dame Kelly Holmes b. 1970	04:55	19:04	10:49	23:11	14:15	03:50	
20	Sa	Nicholas Lyndhurst b. 1961	04:53	19:06	11:49	—	15:25	04:00	
21	Su	Queen Eliz. II b.1926	04:51	19:07	00:03	12:35	16:35	04:10	
22	M	Passover beg/Earth Day	04:49	19:09	00:46	13:12	17:45	04:19	
23	T	St George/Pr Louis b. 2018	04:47	19:11	01:22	13:45	18:58	04:30	
24	W	Woolworth Bldg op. NYC 1913	04:45	19:12	01:55	14:14	20:14	04:42	
25	Th	Anzac Day	04:43	19:14	02:26	14:43	21:32	04:57	
26	F	Chernobyl disaster 1986	04:41	19:16	02:58	15:15	22:50	05:18	
27	Sa	Betty Boothroyd speaker 1992	04:39	19:17	03:32	15:49	—	05:48	
28	Su	*The Gherkin* op. 2004	04:37	19:19	04:08	16:24	00:02	06:33	
29	M	P William m. Catherine 2011	04:35	19:21	04:46	17:00	01:01	07:34	
30	Tu	Passover ends	04:33	19:22	05:30	17:43	01:44	08:50	

Weather column (running vertical text): Bright and sunny in all parts but mostly cool temperatures with cold nights and a risk of some occasional overnight frost. A rainfall deficit is to be expected at this time.

MOON'S PHASES APRIL 2024			Days	Hours	Mins
	☽	Last Quarter	2	03	14
	●	New Moon	8	18	20
	☾	First Quarter	15	19	13
	○	Full Moon	23	23	48

All times on this page are GMT (Add 1 hr BST)

PREDICTIONS

The New Moon on 8 April falls in Aries in the seventh house at London and in a conjunction with Mercury. Mars and Saturn are in a conjunction in the fifth house at London. The entire UK is in a period of major reorganisation, rebalancing the distribution of power between Westminster, the Sennedd, Holyrood and Stormont. Foreign policy is top of the agenda as the UK attempts to redefine its global role. There is a high chance of new trade deals focusing on food and agricultural products. There may be problems with supply chains at sea and possible naval confrontations. Election fever peaks as the government considers going to the country early.

The Full Moon on 23 April falls in Scorpio on the Midheaven at London. Mars is conjunct Saturn and Neptune in the second house at London. There will be strong opposition to the government and a sense that the will of the people must prevail. There is a high chance of conflict resulting from miscommunication and decisions taken without due regard to circumstances and evidence. High stress erupts in the USA and continues in Russia. We can expect freak weather in the Midwest of the USA.

The Randox *Grand National* may see an 11-year-old favourite first past the post. At Ayr, the *Scottish Grand National* could go to a second favourite.

MAY

For High Water add 5h 30m for Bristol, 4h 23m for Hull, 0h 43m for Leith; subtract 2h 21m for Dublin, 1h 26m for Greenock, 2h 29m for Liverpool.

D of M	D of W	Festivals, Events and Anniversaries	Sun at London		High Water at London Bridge		Moon at London		Wea-ther
			Rises	Sets	am	pm	Rises	Sets	
			h m	h m	h m	h m	h m	h m	
1	W	Act of Union 1707	04:31	19:24	06:22	18:37	02:15	10:16	Cold during the first 7–10 days with overnight frosts. All parts turning mild by the third week leading to a sunny and very warm close with record temperatures in the east and south.
2	Th	Princess Charlotte b. 2015	04:29	19:26	07:31	19:49	02:37	11:45	
3	F	Festival of Britain op. 1951	04:27	19:27	08:57	21:20	02:54	13:13	
4	Sa	Battle of Tewkesbury 1471	04:26	19:29	10:13	22:37	03:08	14:41	
5	Su	Rogation Sunday	04:24	19:31	11:20	23:40	03:20	16:09	
6	M	Charles III c'nation 2023/BH	04:22	19:32	—	12:19	03:33	17:39	
7	Tu	Gary Cooper b. 1901	04:20	19:34	00:34	13:09	03:48	19:11	
8	W	VE Day 1945	04:19	19:35	01:21	13:54	04:07	20:42	
9	Th	Ascension Day	04:17	19:37	02:06	14:36	04:32	22:09	
10	F	National Gallery op. 1824	04:15	19:38	02:49	15:17	05:08	23:23	
11	Sa	*Cats* op. London 1981	04:14	19:40	03:33	15:56	05:58	—	
12	Su	First H-bomb test 1951	04:12	19:42	14:17	16:35	07:03	00:19	
13	M	Stevie Wonder b. 1950	04:11	19:43	05:01	17:14	08:17	00:58	
14	Tu	British Legion founded 1921	04:09	19:45	05:47	17:55	09:33	01:25	
15	W	James Mason b. 1909	04:08	19:46	06:40	18:45	10:49	01:43	
16	Th	Sammy Davis Jnr d. 1990	04:06	19:48	07:42	19:54	12:01	01:57	
17	F	Sandro Botticelli d. 1510	04:05	19:49	08:48	21:10	13:12	02:08	
18	Sa	Pope John Paul II b. 1920	04:03	19:50	09:53	22:16	14:21	02:18	
19	Su	Pentecost	04:02	19:52	10:53	23:13	15:31	02:28	
20	M	Columbus d. 1506	04:01	19:53	11:45	—	16:43	02:38	
21	Tu	Cutty Sark fire 2007	03:59	19:55	00:02	12:29	17:58	02:49	
22	W	Rajiv Gandhi assass. 1991	03:58	19:56	00:44	13:07	19:16	03:03	
23	Th	Vesak Day	03:57	19:57	01:23	13:43	20:35	03:22	
24	F	PM Theresa May resigns 2019	03:56	19:59	02:00	14:19	21:51	03:50	
25	Sa	Edict of Worms 1521	03:55	20:00	02:37	14:56	22:55	04:30	
26	Su	Trinity Sunday	03:54	20:01	03:17	15:34	23:44	05:26	
27	M	Spring bank holiday	03:53	20:03	03:58	16:13	—	06:40	
28	Tu	First Glyndebourne 1934	03:52	20:04	04:41	16:54	00:18	08:04	
29	W	Heysel Stadium riot 1985	03:51	20:05	05:28	17:39	00:43	09:31	
30	Th	Corpus Christi	03:50	20:06	06:22	18:31	01:00	10:58	
31	F	Bolt world record 2008	03:49	20:07	07:27	19:36	01:15	12:24	

			Days	Hours	Mins
MOON'S	☾	Last Quarter	1	11	27
PHASES	●	New Moon	8	03	21
MAY	☽	First Quarter	15	11	48
2024	○	Full Moon	23	13	53
	☾	Last Quarter	30	17	12

All times on this page are GMT (Add 1 hr BST)

PREDICTIONS

The New Moon on 8 May is in Taurus in a conjunction with Jupiter and Uranus. This is a revolutionary moment and the desire for liberation on all levels is strong. We may expect technological breakthroughs, including in space flight along with plans to colonise the Moon and Mars, and developments in sustainable food and life-support systems. The political gear-change in Scotland enters a new phase and it is clear there is no way back to the old balance of power. The SNP will need to broaden its approach to reach the electorate. China reaches maximum planetary stress and will take an increasingly assertive role on the world stage.

The Full Moon on 23 May falls in Sagittarius in the third house in London. The Sun is in the ninth house in a conjunction with Venus and Jupiter. The general mood is hopeful and optimistic, and there is a sense that anything can be achieved. The planetary patterns are generally becoming more relaxed. However, the danger is that complacency can lead to accidents, so diplomacy and proposals for peace must be stepped up. Education is a key priority. The UK property market is generally buoyant but new regulations cause fears of a fresh dip in prices.

At Newmarket, the *2,000 Guineas* may see a colt win, whereas the *1,000 Guineas* may go to a second favourite trained in the North.

JUNE

For High Water add 5h 30m for Bristol, 4h 23m for Hull, 0h 43m for Leith; subtract 2h 21m for Dublin, 1h 26m for Greenock, 2h 29m for Liverpool.

D of M	D of W	Festivals, Events and Anniversaries	Sun at London Rises	Sun at London Sets	High Water at London Bridge am	High Water at London Bridge pm	Moon at London Rises	Moon at London Sets	Weather
			h m	h m	h m	h m	h m	h m	
1	Sa	Sir Frank Whittle b. 1907	03:48	20:08	08:39	20:56	01:27	13:50	A thundery month in most parts with generally changeable weather but regular sunny spells. South and south-east areas may see the warmest overall temperatures.
2	Su	Feast of St Elmo	03:47	20:09	09:47	22:08	01:40	15:16	
3	M	World Bicycle Day	03:47	20:10	10:53	23:12	01:53	16:44	
4	Tu	Princess Lilibet b. 2021	03:46	20:11	11:54	—	02:10	18:14	
5	W	Lizzie Borden trial 1893	03:46	20:12	00:10	12:47	02:31	19:42	
6	Th	D-Day 1944	03:45	20:13	01:02	13:34	03:02	21:02	
7	F	Louis XIV crowned 1654	03:44	20:14	01:49	14:17	03:45	22:06	
8	Sa	*1984* published 1949	03:44	20:15	02:35	14:59	04:44	22:53	
9	Su	George Stephenson b. 1781	03:44	20:16	03:19	15:39	05:56	23:25	
10	M	Prince Philip b. 1921	03:43	20:16	04:04	16:17	07:13	23:47	
11	Tu	Shavuot begins	03:43	20:17	04:46	16:54	08:30	—	
12	W	Sir Billy Butlin d. 1980	03:43	20:18	05:28	17:32	09:45	00:03	
13	Th	Shavuot ends	03:43	20:18	06:12	18:12	10:56	00:15	
14	F	Boy George b. 1961	03:42	20:19	07:00	19:01	12:06	00:25	
15	Sa	Trooping the Colour	03:42	20:19	07:55	20:07	13:16	00:35	
16	Su	Father's Day	03:42	20:20	08:53	21:17	14:26	00:44	
17	M	Apartheid abolished 1991	03:42	20:20	09:50	22:18	15:39	00:55	
18	Tu	Delia Smith b. 1941	03:42	20:20	10:47	23:14	16:56	01:08	
19	W	Boris Johnson b. 1964	03:42	20:21	11:41	—	18:15	01:25	
20	Th	Summer solstice 21 50	03:43	20:21	00:06	12:31	19:33	01:49	
21	F	Prince William b. 1982	03:43	20:21	00:54	13:17	20:44	02:24	
22	Sa	George V crowned 1911	03:43	20:21	01:39	14:01	21:39	03:15	
23	Su	International Widows Day	03:43	20:21	02:24	14:44	22:19	04:24	
24	M	Juan Fangio b. 1911	03:44	20:21	03:08	15:26	22:47	05:47	
25	Tu	Michael Jackson d. 2009	03:44	20:21	03:53	16:08	23:07	07:16	
26	W	Bicycle patented 1819	03:45	20:21	04:38	16:49	23:22	08:45	
27	Th	Stratford Martyrs burned 1556	03:45	20:21	05:25	17:32	23:35	10:12	
28	F	Deborah James d. 2022	03:46	20:21	06:15	18:20	23:47	11:37	
29	Sa	UK Armed Forces Day	03:46	20:21	07:12	19:17	—	13:02	
30	Su	Night of Long Knives 1934	03:47	20:20	08:15	20:27	00:00	14:28	

MOON'S PHASES JUNE 2024			Days	Hours	Mins
	●	New Moon	6	12	37
	☽	First Quarter	14	05	18
	○	Full Moon	22	01	07
	☾	Last Quarter	28	21	53

All times on this page are GMT (Add 1 hr BST)

PREDICTIONS

The New Moon on 6 June falls in Gemini in a conjunction with Venus in the ninth house at London. Neptune is exactly on the descendent. A line-up of five planets in Gemini indicates a global shift of mood to greater flexibility. New initiatives launched at this time are unlikely to fail. The upside is that initial failure gives more time for revision and refinement, and ultimate success. Key political issues concern control of the internet and social media. Efforts to restrict access will generally be unsuccessful.

The Full Moon on 22 June is in Capricorn on the ninth house cusp at London in a challenging square to the Moon. Constitutional and legal reforms predominate, especially concerning miscarriages of justice in family law and property rights. There may be a major constitutional convention, exploring changes in the electoral and voting system, including electronic voting, and devolved powers. There will be arguments about whether to reform or abolish the House of Lords. The higher education sector will also be subject to new regulations with attempts to blur the boundary between vocational and academic qualifications. The Russian government enters a period of confidence, finding new allies on the world stage.

The Epsom *Oaks* may see a second favourite as winner, whilst the Epsom *Derby* may go to a surprise outsider.

JULY

For High Water add 5h 30m for Bristol, 4h 23m for Hull, 0h 43m for Leith; subtract 2h 21m for Dublin, 1h 26m for Greenock, 2h 29m for Liverpool.

D of M	D of W	Festivals, Events and Anniversaries	Sun at London Rises	Sun at London Sets	High Water at London Bridge am	High Water at London Bridge pm	Moon at London Rises	Moon at London Sets	Weather
			h m	h m	h m	h m	h m	h m	
1	M	Princess Diana b. 1961	03:47	20:20	09:19	21:39	00:15	15:55	
2	Tu	Ernest Hemingway d. 1961	03:48	20:20	10:24	22:47	00:34	17:22	
3	W	Jim Morrison d. 1971	03:49	20:19	11:30	23:52	01:00	18:44	
4	Th	US Independence Day	03:50	20:19	—	12:30	01:38	19:54	
5	F	First BBC TV news 1954	03:51	20:18	00:50	13:21	02:30	20:47	
6	Sa	Islamic New Year	03:51	20:18	01:41	14:06	03:37	21:24	
7	Su	7/7 terrorist attacks 2005	03:52	20:17	02:27	14:47	04:53	21:49	
8	M	Hugo Boss b. 1885	03:53	20:16	03:11	15:25	06:11	22:07	
9	Tu	Barbara Cartland b. 1901	03:54	20:16	03:51	16:00	07:27	22:21	
10	W	Paris Metro opened 1900	03:55	20:15	04:29	16:33	08:40	22:32	
11	Th	World Population Day	03:56	20:14	05:04	17:06	09:51	22:42	
12	F	Orangemen's Day (hol) NI	03:58	20:13	05:38	17:39	11:01	22:51	
13	Sa	World Cup instituted 1930	03:59	20:12	06:14	18:14	12:10	23:01	
14	Su	Bastille Day (France)	04:00	20:11	06:53	18:55	13:22	23:13	
15	M	St Swithin's Day	04:01	20:10	07:42	19:51	14:36	23:28	
16	Tu	Richard II crowned 1377	04:02	20:09	08:44	21:16	15:53	23:48	
17	W	HM Queen Camilla b. 1947	04:03	20:08	09:52	22:28	17:12	—	
18	Th	Nelson Mandela Day	04:05	20:07	10:58	23:31	18:26	00:17	
19	F	George IV crowned 1821	04:06	20:06	—	12:01	19:29	01:01	
20	Sa	FIFA Women's World Cup 2023	04:07	20:05	00:29	12:56	20:15	02:03	
21	Su	Battersea Bridge op. 1890	04:09	20:03	01:22	13:46	20:48	03:23	
22	M	Prince George b. 2013	04:10	20:02	02:11	14:31	21:11	04:52	
23	Tu	Daniel Radcliffe b. 1989	04:11	20:01	02:57	15:14	21:28	06:24	
24	W	Amelia Earhart b. 1898	04:13	19:59	03:43	15:56	21:42	07:55	
25	Th	Feast of St James	04:14	19:58	04:27	16:36	21:54	09:23	
26	F	Olympics 2024 open in Paris	04:16	19:57	05:11	17:17	22:07	10:49	
27	Sa	Bernard Cribbins d. 2022	04:17	19:55	05:58	18:01	22:21	12:16	
28	Su	Churchill retires 1964	04:18	19:54	06:47	18:51	22:39	13:43	
29	M	Vincent van Gogh d. 1890	04:20	19:52	07:43	19:55	23:02	15:10	
30	Tu	Last Top of the Pops 2006	04:21	19:51	08:46	21:10	23:35	16:33	
31	W	Weimar Republic est. 1919	04:23	19:49	09:55	22:25	—	18:46	

Across Britain, warm, thundery days reaching record high temperatures are followed by cooler, sometimes rainy, weather, picking up towards the end of the month.

MOON'S PHASES JULY 2024		Days	Hours	Mins
●	New Moon	5	22	57
☽	First Quarter	13	22	48
○	Full Moon	21	10	17
☾	Last Quarter	28	02	51

All times on this page are GMT (Add 1 hr BST)

PREDICTIONS

The New Moon on the 5 July falls in Cancer. Mars and Uranus are in a conjunction in the second house at London and Neptune is on the ascendant conjunct the fixed star Scheat. This is not the best time to launch new initiatives; caution and forward planning is favoured. Unforeseen circumstances are likely to derail what otherwise seem like certain successes. The financial system will be subject to some short-term turbulence but is essentially stable. There is a risk of outbreaks of violence in the Middle East, focusing on Israel and Lebanon, drawing in Egypt

The Full Moon on 21 July falls in Capricorn in a conjunction with Pluto. Neptune is on the descendent at London and Mars and Uranus are on the ninth house cusp. This is a very volatile moment and peacekeeping efforts must be the redoubled. Initiatives to resolve the Ukrainian war are launched by eastern European countries led by Poland and Hungary. Thailand is ready for a change of government. There is a high chance of extremist outbreaks in the USA. Planetary tensions focus on east and southern Africa, Tanzania, Uganda, Kenya, Zambia and Zimbabwe, with general pressure across the board for change in the top leadership of all these countries.

The QIPCO *King George VI and Queen Elizabeth Stakes* at Ascot may see a horse carrying 9st 1lb romp to victory.

TENSION DROPS

AUGUST

For High Water add 5h 30m for Bristol, 4h 23m for Hull, 0h 43m for Leith; subtract 2h 21m for Dublin, 1h 26m for Greenock, 2h 29m for Liverpool.

D of M	D of W	Festivals, Events and Anniversaries	Sun at London Rises	Sun at London Sets	High Water at London Bridge am	High Water at London Bridge pm	Moon at London Rises	Moon at London Sets	Weather
			h m	h m	h m	h m	h m	h m	
1	Th	Berlin Olympics op. 1936	04:24	19:47	11:11	23:40	00:22	18:43	A further burst of summer will last for some 16 days, then the weather turns temporarily changeable and cooler. Best conditions in south and west. Fresher in the east.
2	F	William II d.1100	04:26	19:46	—	12:17	01:23	19:24	
3	Sa	Stanley Baldwin b. 1967	04:27	19:44	00:43	13:10	02:36	19:53	
4	Su	Duchess of Sussex b. 1981	04:29	19:42	01:34	13:54	03:54	20:13	
5	M	Bank holiday (Scotland)	04:30	19:40	02:18	14:32	05:11	20:28	
6	Tu	Lucille Ball b. 1911	04:32	19:39	02:57	15:06	06:25	20:39	
7	W	Oliver Hardy d. 1957	04:34	19:37	03:32	15:37	07:37	20:49	
8	Th	Olivia Newton-John d. 2022	04:35	19:35	04:03	16:07	08:47	20:59	
9	F	John Dryden b. 1631	04:37	19:33	04:33	16:37	09:56	21:08	
10	Sa	Treaty of Nonsuch 1585	04:38	19:31	05:02	17:06	11:07	21:19	
11	Su	Olympics 2024 close in Paris	04:40	19:29	05:32	17:36	12:19	21:32	
12	M	Wililam Blake d. 1827	04:41	19:27	06:04	18:11	13:34	21:49	
13	Tu	Florence Nightingale d. 1910	04:43	19:25	06:43	18:56	14:51	22:13	
14	W	VJ Day 1945	04:45	19:24	07:33	19:58	16:07	22:49	
15	Th	Princess Royal b. 1950	04:46	19:22	08:48	21:41	17:14	23:41	
16	F	Boscastle flood 2004	04:48	19:20	10:18	23:00	18:07	—	
17	Sa	Thierry Henry b.1977	04:49	19:18	11:33	—	18:46	00:53	
18	Su	Robert Redford b. 1937	04:51	19:15	00:07	12:35	19:13	02:19	
19	M	Helium discovered 1868	04:53	19:13	01:04	13:26	19:32	03:52	
20	Tu	Darwin in print 1858	04:54	19:11	01:54	14:12	19:47	05:25	
21	W	Princess Margaret b. 1930	04:56	19:09	02:40	14:55	20:00	06:57	
22	Th	First Match of the Day 1964	04:57	19:07	03:24	15:35	20:13	08:27	
23	F	London Blitz began 1940	04:59	19:06	04:07	16:15	20:27	09:57	
24	Sa	Feast of St Bartholomew	05:00	19:03	04:49	16:55	20:43	11:26	
25	Su	Sean Connery b. 1930	05:02	19:01	05:32	17:37	21:05	12:56	
26	M	Bank holiday	05:04	18:59	06:16	18:25	21:35	14:22	
27	Tu	First Guinness Bk Rcrds 1955	05:05	18:56	07:07	19:26	22:17	15:39	
28	W	Leo Tolstoy b. 1828	05:07	18:54	08:09	20:45	23:15	16:42	
29	Th	Motorcycle patent 1885	05:08	18:52	09:26	22:07	—	17:27	
30	F	Mikhail Gorbachev d. 2022	05:10	18:50	10:52	23:28	00:24	17:58	
31	Sa	Princess Diana d. 1997	05:12	18:48	12:00	—	01:40	18:20	

MOON'S PHASES AUGUST 2024		Days	Hours	Mins
●	New Moon	4	11	13
☽	First Quarter	12	15	18
○	Full Moon	19	18	25
☾	Last Quarter	26	09	25

All times on this page are GMT (Add 1 hr BST)

PREDICTIONS

The New Moon on 4 August falls in Leo on the tenth house at London in a harmonious relationship with Mars and Jupiter. In the UK, the government will be strong, boosted by strong financial indications, especially from the tech and communications sectors. There is a chance of peaceful demonstrations turning violent without warning. There are fears of sectarian violence in Northern Ireland and conflict in Scotland. The USA and Russia consider military action in new areas but are also willing to consider peace overtures. Planetary pressures highlight the chance for a fresh economic and political start in Venezuela and Colombia.

The Full Moon on 19 August falls in Aquarius in the first house at London in an opposition to Mercury. The general economic situation eases and share prices in the City of London should enter an upward phase until the end of the year. Challenging times return and there is a very high risk of international arguments and military conflict, partly out of deep-rooted feelings of national pride compounded by a complacent neglect of diplomacy. International tensions can be diffused by seeking solutions which are out of the ordinary. India is facing revolutionary conditions with a major challenge to the government.

At Glorious Goodwood's *King George Qatar Stakes*, a 4-year-old carrying 9st 10lb may be the winner.

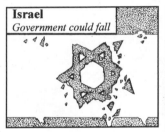

Israel
Government could fall

SEPTEMBER

For High Water add 5h 30m for Bristol, 4h 23m for Hull,
0h 43m for Leith; subtract 2h 21m for Dublin,
1h 26m for Greenock, 2h 29m for Liverpool.

D of M	D of W	Festivals, Events and Anniversaries	Sun at London Rises	Sun at London Sets	High Water at London Bridge am	High Water at London Bridge pm	Moon at London Rises	Moon at London Sets	Weather
			h m	h m	h m	h m	h m	h m	
1	Su	Louis XIV d. 1715	05:13	18:45	00:31	12:52	02:57	18:35	
2	M	Henri Rousseau d. 1910	05:15	18:43	01:19	13:34	04:12	18:48	
3	Tu	Ho Chi Minh d. 1969	05:16	18:41	01:59	14:10	05:25	18:58	
4	W	Napolean III deposed 1870	05:18	18:39	02:34	14:41	06:35	19:09	
5	Th	Louis XIV b. 1638	05:20	18:36	03:05	15:09	07:45	19:16	
6	F	Sir Len Hutton d. 1990	05:21	18:34	03:32	15:37	08:54	19:26	
7	Sa	Elizabeth I b. 1533	05:23	18:32	03:59	16:06	10:06	19:38	
8	Su	Queen Elizabeth II d. 2022	05:24	18:30	04:26	16:35	11:19	19:53	
9	M	Battle of Flodden 1513	05:26	18:27	04:55	17:05	12:35	20:14	
10	Tu	Karl Lagerfeld b.1933	05:28	18:25	05:26	17:39	13:50	20:44	
11	W	9/11 2001	05:29	18:23	06:02	18:22	15:00	21:27	
12	Th	Saragarhi Day	05:31	18:20	06:49	19:21	15:58	22:29	
13	F	Roald Dahl Day	05:32	18:18	07:54	20:56	16:42	23:47	
14	Sa	Feast of the Cross	05:34	18:16	09:37	22:31	17:13	—	
15	Su	Prince Harry b. 1984	05:36	18:14	11:03	23:42	17:35	01:15	
16	M	Mayflower set sail 1620	05:37	18:11	—	12:08	17:52	02:48	
17	Tu	Stirling Moss b. 1929	05:39	18:09	00:40	13:00	18:06	04:21	
18	W	Lunar eclipse 00 41	05:40	18:07	01:31	13:46	18:19	05:53	
19	Th	Funeral of Elizabeth II 2022	05:42	18:04	02:17	14:29	18:32	07:25	
20	F	Premier League formed 1991	05:44	18:02	03:00	15:10	18:47	08:58	
21	Sa	Malta independent 1964	05:45	18:00	03:42	15:51	19:07	10:32	
22	Su	Autumn equinox 13 43	05:47	17:57	04:23	16:32	19:34	12:03	
23	M	Int. Sign Language Day	05:48	17:55	05:03	17:15	20:13	13:27	
24	Tu	Jim Henson b. 1936	05:50	17:53	05:45	18:03	21:06	14:37	
25	W	Michael Douglas b. 1944	05:52	17:50	06:32	19:03	22:13	15:28	
26	Th	RMS *Q. Mary* launched 1934	05:53	17:48	07:31	20:20	23:29	16:03	
27	F	Jesuits founded 1540	05:55	17:46	08:54	21:44	—	16:27	
28	Sa	Shimon Peres d. 2016	05:56	17:44	10:23	23:05	00:46	16:44	
29	Su	Michaelmas	05:58	17:41	11:33	—	02:01	16:57	
30	M	James Dean's car crash 1955	06:00	17:39	00:07	12:24	03:14	17:07	

Weather column (vertical text): Restoring the favourable summer balance, a pleasant but sometimes cool month is likely, the rainfall of short duration. Mostly warm days and cool nights with wind from the west.

MOON'S PHASES SEPTEMBER 2024

		Days	Hours	Mins
●	New Moon	3	01	55
☽	First Quarter	11	06	05
○	Full Moon	18	02	34
☾	Last Quarter	24	18	49

All times on this page are GMT (Add 1 hr BST)

PREDICTIONS

The New Moon on 3 September falls in Virgo on the third house cusp at London, in an opposition to Saturn. Educational and legal affairs are paramount. Communities need to be informed of each other's interests and legal reforms must guarantee that everybody has an equal voice. Practical measures are emphasised, and idealistic solutions are likely to fail. EU countries take steps towards democratic reorganisation, strengthening the power of the European parliament. Israel is in a period of heightened tension, even putting the government at risk. Italy faces governmental change.

The Full Moon on 18 September is an eclipse in Pisces and a conjunction with Neptune. A gradual long-term historic shift is taking place and apparently minor events will add up to a global change of gear. There is a need to find pragmatic solutions and not take stands on principle. The best way forward is to recognise that successful politics requires balance and compromise. The Balkan region faces pressure, and Serbia is at a crossroads, choosing between Russia and the EU. Brazil takes major new steps to protect the Amazon and banishes some international companies from the region.

At Doncaster's *St. Leger*, the winner may be a favoured colt trained in the Midlands. In the *Gold Cup* at Ayr, a jockey weighing in at 9st 4lb may be the victor.

OCTOBER

For High Water add 5h 30m for Bristol, 4h 23m for Hull, 0h 43m for Leith; subtract 2h 21m for Dublin, 1h 26m for Greenock, 2h 29m for Liverpool.

D of M	D of W	Festivals, Events and Anniversaries	Sun at London Rises	Sun at London Sets	High Water at London Bridge am	High Water at London Bridge pm	Moon at London Rises	Moon at London Sets	Weather
			h m	h m	h m	h m	h m	h m	
1	Tu	Walter Matthau b. 1920	06:01	17:37	00:53	13:05	04:25	17:17	
2	W	Eclipse 15 42/Rosh H'ah beg.	06:03	17:34	01:31	13:40	05:34	17:26	
3	Th	OJ Simpson acquitted 1995	06:05	17:32	02:04	14:11	06:44	17:36	
4	F	Rosh Hashanah ends	06:06	17:30	02:33	14:39	07:55	17:47	
5	Sa	Guildford bomb 1974	06:08	17:28	02:59	15:07	09:08	18:00	
6	Su	Fiji a republic 1987	06:10	17:25	03:25	15:37	10:23	18:19	
7	M	Heinrich Himmler b. 1900	06:11	17:23	03:54	16:08	11:38	18:45	
8	Tu	Mini Metro launched 1980	06:13	17:21	04:24	16:41	12:49	19:22	
9	W	Feast of St Denis	06:15	17:19	04:56	17:18	13:51	20:16	
10	Th	World Mental Health Day	06:16	17:17	05:33	18:03	14:38	21:25	
11	F	Yom Kippur	06:18	17:14	06:20	19:02	15:13	22:47	
12	Sa	Salem Witch Trials end 1692	06:20	17:12	07:25	20:30	15:37	23:16	
13	Su	Margaret Thatcher b. 1925	06:21	17:10	09:01	22:02	15:55	—	
14	M	Robbie Coltrane d. 2022	06:23	17:08	10:30	23:13	16:10	01:46	
15	Tu	PG Wodehouse b. 1881	06:25	17:06	11:36	—	16:23	02:16	
16	W	Sukkot begins	06:26	17:04	00:13	12:30	16:36	04:47	
17	Th	Lunar eclipse 11 10	06:28	17:02	01:04	13:18	16:51	06:20	
18	F	Martina Navratilova b. 1956	06:30	16:59	01:51	14:02	17:08	07:55	
19	Sa	Michael Gambon b. 1940	06:32	16:57	02:34	14:45	17:32	09:30	
20	Su	49th Parallel est. 1818	06:33	16:55	03:16	15:28	18:06	11:02	
21	M	Geoff Boycott b. 1940	06:35	16:53	03:57	16:12	18:55	12:21	
22	Tu	Derek Jacobi b. 1938	06:37	16:51	04:37	16:56	19:59	13:22	
23	W	Sukkot ends	06:38	16:49	05:18	17:45	21:14	14:03	
24	Th	United Nations Day	06:40	16:47	06:02	18:42	22:32	14:32	
25	F	Private Eye pub. 1961	06:42	16:45	06:57	19:53	23:49	14:51	
26	Sa	FA founded 1863	06:44	16:43	08:16	21:09	—	15:05	
27	Su	Churchill PM 1951	06:45	16:41	09:39	22:23	01:03	15:16	
28	M	Jerry Lee Lewis d. 2022	06:47	16:40	10:48	23:27	02:14	15:26	
29	Tu	Wall Street crash 1929	06:49	16:38	11:43	—	03:24	15:35	
30	W	Aspirin on sale 1905	06:51	16:36	00:16	12:27	04:33	15:45	
31	Th	Halloween/Diwali	06:52	16:34	00:55	13:05	05:44	15:55	

A late rally in the general weather temperature is likely between the 10th and 20th, following a changeable start. Changeable, windy in the west and north at the end.

MOON'S PHASES OCTOBER 2024		Days	Hours	Mins
●	New Moon	2	18	49
☽	First Quarter	10	18	55
○	Full Moon	17	11	26
☾	Last Quarter	24	08	03

All times on this page are GMT (BST to 26 October + 1 hour)

PREDICTIONS

The New Moon on 2 October falls in Libra in a conjunction with Mercury in the sixth house at London and a square with Mars. Venus is in a harmonious relationship with Saturn. The interplanetary position favours peace and reconciliation, but also complacency. There will be a need to balance competing interests in the UK. There is a recognition of the importance of holistic solutions to healthcare. There may be some discord in the educational sector with possible strikes. Russia enters a major phase of infrastructure investment and reorganisation. Tensions in the USA may boil over ahead of the Presidential election. This is a period determining the country's direction for some years,

The Full Moon on 17 October is an eclipse in Aries and is in a square with Mars and Pluto. A rare cardinal grand Cross connects these planets with the Sun and indicates that this is a time to build new structures for global co-operation and healing. We can expect significant progress towards major agreements including a new financial system that recognises the historic contributions of poorer countries to richer ones. Greece is entering a period of change and economic recovery. West Africa receives global attention with tensions high in Ghana.

At Newmarket's *Cesarewitch Heritage Handicap* victory may go to a horse bearing 8st 3lb.

NOVEMBER

For High Water add 5h 30m for Bristol, 4h 23m for Hull, 0h 43m for Leith; subtract 2h 21m for Dublin, 1h 26m for Greenock, 2h 29m for Liverpool.

D of M	D of W	Festivals, Events and Anniversaries	Sun at London Rises	Sun at London Sets	High Water at London Bridge am	High Water at London Bridge pm	Moon at London Rises	Moon at London Sets	Weather
			h m	h m	h m	h m	h m	h m	
1	F	All Saints' Day	06:54	16:32	01:29	13:39	06:56	16:08	
2	Sa	Day of the Dead, Mexico	06:56	16:30	01:59	14:10	08:11	16:25	
3	Su	Adam Ant b. 1954	06:58	16:29	02:27	14:40	09:27	16:49	
4	M	Diwali ends	07:00	16:27	02:56	15:12	10:40	17:23	
5	Tu	Bonfire Night/US election	07:01	16:25	03:28	15:47	11:45	18:11	
6	W	Sally Field b. 1946	07:03	16:24	04:02	16:25	12:36	19:15	
7	Th	Leslie Phillips d. 2022	07:05	16:22	04:37	17:06	13:14	20:32	
8	F	Margaret Mitchell b. 1900	07:07	16:20	05:17	17:54	13:41	21:56	
9	Sa	Berlin Wall falls 1989	07:08	16:19	06:05	18:53	14:00	23:22	
10	Su	Remembrance Day	07:10	16:17	07:06	20:12	14:15	—	
11	M	Armistice day 1918	07:12	16:16	08:29	21:33	14:29	00:49	
12	Tu	World Pneumonia Day	07:14	16:14	09:55	22:42	14:41	02:16	
13	W	*Fantasia* opened 1940	07:15	16:13	11:03	23:43	14:54	03:44	
14	Th	HM the King b. 1948	07:17	16:11	—	12:01	15:10	05:16	
15	F	Guru Nanak birthday	07:19	16:10	00:38	12:52	15:30	06:50	
16	Sa	Clark Gable d. 1960	07:20	16:09	01:26	13:39	15:59	08:25	
17	Su	Elizabeth I assess. 1558	07:22	16:07	02:11	14:25	16:41	09:53	
18	M	Nadia Sawalha b. 1964	07:24	16:06	02:54	15:10	17:40	11:05	
19	Tu	Sturgeon SNP Leader 2014	07:25	16:05	03:36	15:56	18:53	11:57	
20	W	Pr Elizabeth m. Philip 1947	07:27	16:04	04:17	16:42	20:13	12:31	
21	Th	Birmingham pub bombs 1974	07:29	16:03	04:57	17:29	21:32	12:55	
22	F	Thatcher resigns 1990	07:30	16:02	05:39	18:21	22:49	13:11	
23	Sa	John Major PM 1990	07:32	16:01	06:26	19:20	—	13:24	
24	Su	Hunting Act passed 2004	07:34	16:00	07:28	20:24	00:01	13:34	
25	M	George Best d. 2005	07:35	15:59	08:44	21:27	01:12	13:44	
26	Tu	Tutankhamun found 1922	07:37	15:58	09:51	22:27	02:21	13:53	
27	W	Jimi Hendrix b. 1942	07:38	15:57	10:50	23:23	03:31	14:03	
28	Th	Thanksgiving (USA)	07:40	15:56	11:42	—	04:42	14:15	
29	F	London Brdg attack 2019	07:41	15:55	00:10	12:27	05:57	14:31	
30	Sa	St Andrew's Day	07:42	15:55	00:51	13:07	07:13	14:53	

Weather column note (vertical): Often mild with windy days, sometimes gales, from the start. No early cold spell is likely to follow, but instead continuing mild conditions with mid-month quiet periods.

MOON'S PHASES NOVEMBER 2024

		Days	Hours	Mins
●	New Moon	1	12	47
☽	First Quarter	9	05	55
○	Full Moon	15	21	28
☾	Last Quarter	23	01	27

All times on this page are GMT

PREDICTIONS

The New Moon on 1 November is in Scorpio and the ninth house in London in a harmonious trine with Saturn. Mars is exactly opposed to Pluto and Mercury is exactly opposed to Uranus. Venus is squared to Saturn. The sense of historic change and that the world is turning a corner gets stronger. This is also a moment of great potential risk. Conservative values are favoured, and political priorities must rest on the preservation of everything that is best, along with mutual respect for other countries and communities. The US Presidential election takes place on 5 November amidst an explosive and confrontational atmosphere.

The Full Moon on 15 November falls in Taurus in an exact conjunction with Uranus. Mercury is opposed to Jupiter. There is a sense that the world is coming to the end of a thirty-year phase and the beginning of a new one. Instability continues but tension relaxes and radical solutions to national and international problems are possible. Political initiatives lack a clear focus, and any new arrangements are unlikely to last. Tension in China reaches a new peak with maximum fears of civil unrest and armed confrontation. Expect changes of leadership in Turkey.

A 4-year-old horse carrying 10st 6lb may be the winner at Newbury in the Ladbroke's *Trophy Handicap* steeplechase.

DECEMBER

For High Water add 5h 30m for Bristol, 4h 23m for Hull, 0h 43m for Leith; subtract 2h 21m for Dublin, 1h 26m for Greenock, 2h 29m for Liverpool.

D of M	D of W	Festivals, Events and Anniversaries	Sun at London Rises	Sun at London Sets	High Water London Bridge am	High Water London Bridge pm	Moon at London Rises	Moon at London Sets	Weather
			h m	h m	h m	h m	h m	h m	
1	Su	Advent begins	07:44	15:54	01:27	13:44	08:28	15:23	A rapid change to cold weather is expected by mid-month, then milder for some 7–8 days. Turning windy at the close, with a dip in temperatures and frosty mornings.
2	M	Britney Spears b. 1981	07:45	15:54	02:01	14:20	09:36	16:07	
3	Tu	First heart transplant 1967	07:47	15:53	02:37	14:57	10:33	17:08	
4	W	Ronnie Corbett b. 1930	07:48	15:53	03:13	15:36	11:15	18:22	
5	Th	Kirsty Alley d. 2022	07:49	15:52	03:51	16:17	11:44	19:44	
6	F	Feast of St Nicholas	07:50	15:52	04:29	17:01	12:06	21:09	
7	Sa	Great Storm 1703	07:52	15:52	05:10	17:49	12:22	22:34	
8	Su	Mary Queen Scots b. 1542	07:53	15:51	05:56	18:44	12:35	23:58	
9	M	Ruth Madoc d. 2022	07:54	15:51	06:50	19:51	12:47	—	
10	Tu	Kenneth Branagh b. 1960	07:55	15:51	07:57	21:03	13:00	01:22	
11	W	Willie Rushton d. 1996	07:56	15:51	09:20	22:10	13:14	02:49	
12	Th	Robert Browning d. 1889	07:57	15:51	10:31	23:15	13:31	04:19	
13	F	Drake sails 1577	07:58	15:51	11:34	—	13:55	05:51	
14	Sa	Miranda Hart b. 1972	07:59	15:51	00:14	12:32	14:30	07:22	
15	Su	Tower of Pisa reopens 2001	08:00	15:51	01:06	13:23	15:20	08:42	
16	M	Pilgrim Fathers landed 1620	08:00	15:51	01:54	14:12	16:28	09:44	
17	Tu	Dominic Lawson b. 1956	08:01	15:52	02:38	14:59	17:47	10:26	
18	W	Zsa Zsa Gabor d. 2016	08:02	15:52	03:21	15:45	19:09	10:55	
19	Th	*Rimet* trophy stolen 1983	08:02	15:52	04:01	16:30	20:29	11:15	
20	F	John Steinbeck d. 1968	08:03	15:53	04:40	17:12	21:44	11:29	
21	Sa	Winter solstice 09 19	08:03	15:53	05:17	17:54	22:56	11:40	
22	Su	George Eliot d. 1880	08:04	15:54	05:54	18:38	—	11:50	
23	M	*Emma* published 1815	08:04	15:54	06:36	19:27	00:07	12:00	
24	Tu	Christmas Eve	08:05	15:55	07:31	20:23	01:16	12:10	
25	W	Christmas Day	08:05	15:56	08:43	21:20	02:27	12:21	
26	Th	Boxing Day	08:05	15:56	09:50	22:19	03:40	12:35	
27	F	Benazir Bhutto assass. 2007	08:05	15:57	10:51	23:18	04:55	12:54	
28	Sa	Westminster Ab'y con. 1065	08:06	15:58	11:48	—	06:11	13:21	
29	Su	Vivienne Westwood d. 2022	08:06	15:59	00:13	12:39	07:23	14:00	
30	M	Battle of Wakefield 1460	08:06	16:00	01:01	13:24	08:25	14:56	
31	Tu	New Year's Eve/Hogmanay	08:06	16:01	01:44	14:07	08:13	16:07	

MOON'S			Days	Hours	Mins
MOON'S	●	New Moon	1	06	21
PHASES	☽	First Quarter	8	15	26
DECEMBER	○	Full Moon	15	09	01
2024	☾	Last Quarter	22	22	18
	●	New Moon	30	22	26

All times on this page are GMT

PREDICTIONS

The New Moon on 1 December falls in Sagittarius. Mercury is opposed to Jupiter and Mars opposed to Pluto. The short-term cycle shows an increase in tension and minor accidents that could trigger wider conflict. EU countries will be split over fundamental issues, but agreement will be reached by the end of the year. The threat of civil unrest in China continues.

The Full Moon on 15 December falls in Gemini in an exact square to Neptune. This is a moment which favours religious traditions and faith leaders who can offer inspirational leadership where conventional politics fails. Health matters remain a high priority with concern over mental health spending. There will be constitutional reform in Russia, with likely changes in the senior leadership. Globally Mexico, India and Japan face changes of leadership.

The New Moon on 30 December falls in Capricorn in the fourth house at London. Jupiter is on the Midheaven in an opposition to Mercury. This is a moment of optimism, but also of confrontation. People who think that victory is assured will make serious errors. Careful thought and planning are required at all levels of society. It is therefore best to delay action until the new year.

Ladbroke's *King George VI Chase* at Kempton may go to a 6-year-old second favourite. A 7-year-old carrying 9st could take the *Welsh Grand National* at Chepstow.

Old Moore calculates your own birth chart

Your very own personal horoscope by **Old Moore**

The timeless wisdom of **Old Moore** *can now be interpreted by computer – to give you an astounding wealth of insights and revelations.*

At last, the huge analytical power of the computer has been harnessed to the legendary forecasting skills of **Old Moore**.

By revealing the mysteries held within your own astrological chart, you will gain a unique insight into yourself and find a new path to your future which you yourself can influence.

It is based on the **Old Moore** prediction system, which has proved to be uniquely successful and accurate for over three hundred years.

Now it focuses entirely on *YOU*. The result is your very own *character profile and forecast horoscope* for the next twelve months.

Send off the coupon below with your remittance of £20.00, and enjoy a unique view of your future.

12-month Horoscope Book – personal to you – for only £20.00 INCLUDING P&P.

✳ **Most detailed astral reading of its kind.**

✳ **CHARACTER PROFILE explores the depths of your true self.**

✳ **PERSONAL FORECAST predicts ways to improve your happiness and success.**

✳ **In a tradition of accurate forecasting since 1697.**

YOUR DATE WITH DESTINY...

UNIQUE GIFT IDEA – SEND THIS COUPON NOW!

*Your **Old Moore Personal Horoscope** costs just £20.00 (Please allow 28 days for delivery)*

Name ....

Address ....

....

Postcode ....

Telephone ....

Email ....

Date and year of birth ....

Time of birth (if known) ....

Place of birth ....

Use your credit card to order online at www.foulsham.com and enter your date, time and place of birth on the order form.

Or send this completed form to
W. Foulsham & Co. Ltd, Personal Horoscopes, The Old Barrel Store, Drayman's Lane, Marlow, Bucks SL7 2FF.

Please print clearly in BLOCK CAPITALS.

Make cheques payable to W. Foulsham & Co. Ltd.

If you prefer not to receive mailings from companies other than those connected to Old Moore, please tick the box ☐

Rachel Reeves

© Imageplotter/Alamy Stock Photo

Rachel Reeves is one of the longest serving and most competent of the Labour party shadow ministers in the House of Commons. Although we do not have access to her time of birth, her natal chart shows her to be strongly tied to the zodiac sign of Aquarius, where her Sun, Mercury and Mars were positioned at the time of her birth. This makes Rachel a good communicator, supports her overall intelligence and inclines her towards a conciliatory approach in her dealings with others.

Reeves was born in London on 13 February 1979 but her life these days is split between the capital and the northern city of Leeds, for which she has been an MP since 2010. Having excelled during her education, Rachel contested several Parliamentary seats before securing that of Leeds West. The tenacity of her birth chart, which is mainly based on Air- and Earth-sign planetary positions, ensured that she would eventually reach her objective of a seat at Westminster and that she would soon secure high-ranking positions in the Labour shadow cabinet. Reeves enjoyed a number of important positions before rising to the position of Shadow Chancellor of the Exchequer in May 2021.

Bearing in mind all the Aquarius in her birth chart, it is not surprising that Rachel Reeves has managed to avoid controversy during her career as a Member of Parliament, though with the Moon in Virgo and Venus in Capricorn it is certain she can dig her heels in when necessary and that she takes a long-term view of her political career. Slowly but surely, and at the same time not without a touch of genius, she has climbed the ladder of influence. She has made her political moderation work well in her favour and on behalf of her constituents.

Reeves was not a natural supporter of Jeremy Corbyn but she enjoys the confidence of Sir Keir Starmer and she seems to be set fair to maintain her high standing in the Labour Party. With the strength in her natal chart only increasing, there is every chance that in the fullness of time Rachel Reeves could lead the Labour Party and it is not beyond the realms of possibility that one day she could become Prime Minister. Reeves has what it takes in the strength of her personality to bring opposing factions together and it is partly this skill that will make her a candidate for greatness in the fullness of time. Balancing the needs of a family life with those imposed on her by constant travel and the demands of her career, Rachel Reeves will focus on the job in hand and only grow in stature. She is one of the mainstays of a gradually maturing Labour front bench.

James Norton

© Katie Collins/Alamy Stock Photo

Actor James Norton will probably be most familiar to viewers of the television series *Happy Valley* in which he played villain Tommy Lee Royce. Although Norton had appeared in numerous roles on television and in films before *Happy Valley*, which first aired in 2014, Tommy Lee Royce was Norton's breakout role, which brought him to the attention of the public.

James Geoffrey Ian Norton was born on 18 July 1985 in London. He spent his early years in North Yorkshire, a place that has remained of tremendous importance to him. He attended the prestigious Roman Catholic school at Ampleforth in Yorkshire, then studied theology at Fitzwilliam College Cambridge before going on to RADA (Royal Academy of Dramatic Arts) on a three-year course which he never finished, choosing instead to take his first acting role.

James Norton's birth chart is both complex and fascinating. At the time of his birth, Norton has three planets, Sun, Moon and Mars, all in the watery zodiac sign of Cancer. Such is the sensitivity of his chart that Norton might equally have found his future in the Church. However, with Venus in Gemini he possesses the chameleon-like ability to change his colours and to convincingly assume the mantle of a multitude of individuals radically different from his own persona. With Jupiter in airy Aquarius and Mercury in fiery Leo, James Norton was gifted with everything necessary to walk the boards and to stand in front of the camera. He is a man born to act.

In his personal life, Norton plays his cards close to his chest. He has been engaged for some time to actress Imogen Pools but it is likely that, for the time being at least, his commitment to performance will be his major consideration. This is because Norton is, in a sense, wedded to his career. As a result, and on account of his undeniable talent, we are likely to see him appearing in ever more prestigious roles, both on film and television. James Norton is destined to achieve all manner of honours on both sides of the Atlantic and because of the undoubted humanity of all his Cancerian qualities, he is also likely to work hard to help others achieve their objectives in life and may well become something of a role model later in his life. Although it may surprise even him right now, it is not unlikely that in the fullness of time Norton will turn once again to the religion that surrounded him in his early life.

James Norton may surprise us with some of the decisions he chooses to make in the future, but he has the knack of making good choices and the unique properties of his chart reveal that he will prosper from most of them.

LIBRA BORN PEOPLE
Birthdays: 24 September to 23 October inclusive
Planet: Venus. Birthstone: Opal. Lucky day: Friday

Keynote for the Year: *Prepare for a year of hard work, when there will be much to organise. Trends also indicate financial benefits, possibly arising through any type of partnership.*

JANUARY: MAIN TRENDS: 11–12 Any feeling of stagnation at work will cease and you will instinctively know to act decisively to resolve problems quickly. **13–14** Although you may have business negotiations to handle, you will get the best from personal and family matters so reserve some quality time for them. **19–20** Be prepared to work long and hard and throw your energies into going for what you want, Play hard, too! **KEY DATES: HIGHS 3–5** Focus on getting the right results and you should win out over your competition. **LOWS 16–17** Prepare for some challenges, and for things to get off to a slow start.

FEBRUARY: MAIN TRENDS: 11–12 You may be in an insular mood, but this may not be a bad thing – a time of retreat can also be a time of renewal. **17–18** As thing seem to be going your way at home and at work, this is the time to create your own luck. **19–20** Be aware of your limitations and work patiently within them. Don't be too impetuous – there may be pitfalls later. **KEY DATES: HIGHS 1; 27–28** A planetary 'pick up' which gears you up for just about anything life can throw at you. **LOWS 13–14** Plans may be slow moving if they even get off the ground at all. Be aware that this is a temporary phase.

MARCH: MAIN TRENDS: 4–5 A favourable period for big gatherings; you should now get the best from both worlds – work and social. **10–11** Understand your priorities and get to the root of a personal matter involving a partner or your finances. **21–22** Playing the prima donna may lead to some success – you enjoy feeling appreciated and loved ones may be keen to oblige. **KEY DATES: HIGHS 25–26** Romance and social life is positively highlighted – take a leading role in whatever is happening now. **LOWS 12–13** In low spirits, you may also be lagging in confidence – keep a low profile and attend to any unfinished business.

APRIL: MAIN TRENDS: 1–2 The domestic scene may be busier and more active now. Career wise, extra demands may lead to some disorganisation. **20–21** Trends suggest you need to beware of shady types and putting trust in the wrong people; 'operating under misconceptions' is the key phrase here. **24–25** You could be wondering about past choices, but this isn't the time to be regretting former decisions and, remember, things won't always stay the same. **KEY DATES: HIGHS 22–23** Optimism and decisive action bring you the chance to make long lasting change. **LOWS 8–9** If you feel life is against you, pace yourself as your energy is low.

MAY: MAIN TRENDS: 2–4 Trends place the spotlight on communication, which may mean that good news is on its way. You may be able to share it with colleagues. **9–10** There are people around you who can lighten your life and bring high spirits to keep you moving forward happily. **21–22** A positive trend for work and finance. Focus on building steadily for the short-term future. **KEY DATES: HIGHS 19–20** A little luck is indicated in your chart, and your social life may be exceptionally busy so approach invitations with optimism. **LOWS 5–6** It's almost certain that you will have to put a certain matter to rest before you can properly relax.

JUNE: MAIN TRENDS: 11–13 Don't become too concerned with the minutiae of material life with its routines and responsibilities, and especially avoid worrying too much. **18–19** An inspiring day is forecast, especially socially, but anything involving co-operation with others should be rewarding and informative. **21–22** If you have a new idea, especially related to something potentially lucrative, trends suggest this is a good time to put it into operation – as long as you're not taking any big risks. **KEY DATES: HIGHS 15–17** Act promptly and take the initiative on any course of action. **LOWS 2–3; 30** Keep a low profile and ride out the low phase.

JULY: MAIN TRENDS: 1–2 In a decisive mood, you should find it easy to accomplish your aims in your preferred manner. **15–16** A great time to spend at home – you will benefit from the sense of belonging and could take on a supportive role in the family. **21–22** The planets increase your skill and confidence to tackle issues in your short-term future. Whilst you will take the initiative in most situations today, a certain amount of caution is needed. **KEY DATES: HIGHS 12–14** Combative and to-the-point now, you should see off your competition during this dynamic phase. **LOWS 26–27** Don't think you have all the answers – there is always something unexpected around the corner.

AUGUST: MAIN TRENDS: 7–8 Happy and emotionally content, you will take enjoyment from your home and pleasure in your roots at this time. **18–19** Trends increase your ego now, so beware of taking yourself too much for granted in dealings with others, especially in personal relationships. **24–26** Emotional relationships should now be fulfilling. For some Librans, there may also be a brand-new love interest. **KEY DATES: HIGHS 9–10** Go for what you want during the monthly high. **LOWS 22–23** Expect a dreary feeling, and a short time when it is easy to lose your way. This will soon pass.

SEPTEMBER: MAIN TRENDS: 3–4 Your powerful personality is on display and others can't fail to be impressed; a plan of yours, whether financial or personal, could work out well. **7–8** A good time to begin a new relationship as trends enhance your attractiveness and others tend to enjoy your company. **22–23** An influence indicating keen powers of observation and good judgement. You should possess good communication skills and also enjoy travel. **KEY DATES: HIGHS 5–7** Success may come easily as you thrive in the company of your superiors and have their support. **LOWS 19–20** Don't rush to solve a problem and be especially careful with your money now.

OCTOBER: MAIN TRENDS: 4–5 A moderately positive time domestically, but if you're trying to change someone's mind at home, stay neutral and allow them to make their own choice. **18–19** You will communicate well with others who have a real appreciation for your ideas. **23–24** Participating in group events or working as part of a team may lead to some social benefits. **KEY DATES: HIGHS 2–3** This influence often signifies some kind of lucky break, particularly in personal matters. Look out for it! **LOWS 16–17** Not everything will run exactly to plan, but a short setback won't mean your plans are spoilt.

NOVEMBER: MAIN TRENDS: 12–13 Pressures at home may be rather demanding and lead to some tense situations – clear these up as soon as possible. **16–17** Your professional life is positively highlighted and trends suggest that making effective change here should become much easier than of late. **21–22** This influence suggests strong intuition about being in the right place at the right time. Think carefully before you make any financial move, though. **KEY DATES: HIGHS 26–27** You enjoy a warm and optimistic outlook during this lucky influence. **LOWS 13–14** Energy may be in short supply so pace yourself and get some rest.

DECEMBER: MAIN TRENDS: 9–10 Trends suggest you'll have things on your mind, and this is an excellent time to discuss them with friends and get them out in the open. **12–13** Some might consider your style rather impulsive, yet a positive attitude coupled with action – the surprise attack! – can bring untold rewards. **21–22** Partnerships should prove very fulfilling, whether with friends or someone closer. A great time for getting out and about. **KEY DATES: HIGHS 23–24** If you have time before Christmas, finish something you've previously put off. **LOWS 10–11** The road ahead may be full of pitfalls so keep to the well-trodden path during this taxing phase.

SCORPIO BORN PEOPLE
Birthdays: 24 October to 22 November inclusive
Planets: Mars, Pluto. Birthstone: Topaz. Lucky day: Tuesday

Keynote for the Year: *One-to-one relationships are enhanced by expansive, lucky Jupiter this year but, despite this, you may feel that an element of romance is missing. Focus on the good times.*

JANUARY: MAIN TRENDS: 13–14 Important news received now may require immediate action – use your alert mind for some fast thinking to help things turn out well. **16–17** Under this influence you may lack the motivation to get things done, so this is an excellent time to spend with loved ones, giving back and catching up. **21–22** Prepare to need to compromise in a potentially volatile personal situation. **KEY DATES: HIGHS 6–7** You're at your best, emotionally, physically, mentally, so make the most of it! **LOWS 18–20** If there are certain compromises you're not prepared to make, work independently.

FEBRUARY: MAIN TRENDS: 4–5 Trends suggest that domestic activities will be very enjoyable so make time for them. **7–8** Do whatever it takes to reach out to your partner or loved ones. Perhaps consider entertaining others at home. **20–21** Trends enhance your attractiveness to others and strengthen your desire for love, but creativity and a healthy self-image are strong, too. **KEY DATES: HIGHS 2–3** Motivated and in good spirits, you should be able to accomplish a lot during this phase. **LOWS 15–16** Take care over everyday difficulties and stresses related to any current goals and avoid overdoing things during this low phase.

MARCH: MAIN TRENDS: 18–19 Make use of your considerable charm and you should find you are of genuine interest to those around you – being on the same wavelength as others is truly rewarding. **20–21** Trends indicate a successful period professionally when you should make good progress. The more ambitious you are, the better. **22–24** You may make important contacts at work as colleagues and managers are generally cooperative and helpful. **KEY DATES: HIGHS 1–2; 27–29** Trends suggest that someone may show some special interest in you! **LOWS 13–14** You may lack the initiative to assert yourself or make decisions. Don't be afraid to take a compliant and passive role.

APRIL: MAIN TRENDS: 1–2 Something you hear at work could prove decidedly useful, whether you use the information now, or save it for later. **3–5** Financially and materially this is a good time to get the kind of help you need, no matter what kind of situation you're in. **22–23** You may find that some positive thinking helps you to move ahead but be sure not to force any projects before they are ready. **KEY DATES: HIGHS 24–25** You are energetic and competitive now and enjoy increased vitality and self-confidence. **LOWS 9–11** Your powers are limited and your influence over others minimal. Bearing this in mind may help you avoid trouble.

MAY: MAIN TRENDS: 5–6 How you get along with others is always a factor in any enterprise, but your main talent now is your skill at bargaining and negotiation. **19–20** A break from routine may do you some good and some meditation may remind you that emotional matters are as important as anything else in life. **27–28** A conversation with friends or colleagues could be stimulating and productive. A short trip or intellectual discussion may be on the agenda. **KEY DATES: HIGHS 21–22** Use your ingenuity to get things to go your way. **LOWS 7–8** Consider streamlining your life now and keep things simple. Live in the moment.

JUNE: MAIN TRENDS: 5–6 The spotlight is on creative activity – you need to be yourself and show the world what you're made of. **19–20** A romantic and light-hearted period replaces all else and you may feel confident that your relationship is on a secure footing. **22–23** For you, feelings are important for your personal development. Some people may view this as overly sentimental, but your opinion is what counts. **KEY DATES: HIGHS 17–18** Focus exclusively on one goal and you should have the skill to make it happen. **LOWS 3–4; 30** This won't be your luckiest period so set some time aside for rest and reflection.

JULY: MAIN TRENDS: 4–6 The right time to be pushy and to move forward in your career. You've all the drive and energy you need and should find it easy to channel it. **22–23** Prepare to use your personal skills as you enjoy the centre of attention. At work, you may convince a superior that you're the one they need. **26–27** Avoid any impatience to get ahead of the field – it could have a negative effect on your colleagues. **KEY DATES: HIGHS 15–16** News concerning a recent ambition may be encouraging and enjoyable. **LOWS 1–2; 28–29** A time best used for contemplation and regaining your strength; don't be overconcerned with maintaining performance levels.

AUGUST: MAIN TRENDS: 1–2 If you need to usher in new changes in your life, or find information about someone you know, be guided by feelings that go beyond logic. **9–10** There is a danger you could become over obsessed with certain matters, but it is possible to use this instinct positively to remove something unnecessary in your life. **21–23** Trends highlight communications, so conversation, debate and fact-finding should provide the most pleasure. **KEY DATES: HIGHS 11–12** Take the initiative – a snap decision may be luckier than you'd expected. **LOWS 24–25** Get as much rest as you can during this planetary low patch.

SEPTEMBER: MAIN TRENDS: 2–4 A time when you can move ahead successfully, but make sure to complete the important things first and save the fun for later. **22–23** Don't go to great lengths to please others; this will be an impossible task. Put simply, you must avoid ending up as the doormat. **26–27** A positive influence for all social matters, but one-to-one relationships should be most supportive and provide your most rewarding moments. **KEY DATES: HIGHS 7–9** A little cautious gamble may pay dividends now – expect positive results from the business of the day. **LOWS 20–21** Suspend any major decision making and indulge yourself a little.

OCTOBER: MAIN TRENDS: 2–3 Trends bring a real boost to personal relationships, although pretty much anyone you encounter should be warm and friendly. **16–17** It will be best to stay in and soak up family life, if you can. Your home is more special than ever to you under this influence. **23–25** As the Sun moves into your sign, you get much more from your efforts. Forget modest achievement and raise your ambitions. **KEY DATES: HIGHS 4–6** Explore new interests and expect some satisfying results now. **LOWS 18–19** There may be various limitations to contend with today, either professional or personal. Pace yourself.

NOVEMBER: MAIN TRENDS. 4–6 You may feel the need to express certain strong opinions; remember though, that it's the manner of expression that counts. **12–13** The odd trick or two up your sleeve may see you making progress as your talent for persuasion is strong now. **21–22** Let your light shine today, whether in encounters with others or creative pursuits. You should easily make an impression. **KEY DATES: HIGHS 1–2; 28–29** Your chart reveals that you have the foresight to go in the right direction, so be ready to heed the call. **LOWS 14–15** A low-key phase when things slow down, but bear in mind that what you lose in some areas, you gain in others.

DECEMBER: MAIN TRENDS: 1–2 Your most fulfilling moments are now enjoyed at home. An issue from the past may help you put some of the present into perspective. **19–20** Trends may now help you to bring a certain idea to a satisfactory conclusion, particularly regarding a financial ambition. Act decisively, but carefully. **22–23** Personal matters bring out the best in you, and there is emotional support when it comes to anything preying on your mind. **KEY DATES: HIGHS 25–27** Prepare for some nice surprises this Christmas and expect the unexpected! **LOWS 12–13** Be adaptable and self-disciplined, and you should ride out the low phase easily.

SAGITTARIUS BORN PEOPLE
Birthdays: 23 November to 21 December inclusive
Planet: Jupiter. Birthstone: Turquoise. Lucky day: Thursday

Keynote for the Year: *Trends influencing work and health are boosted for the next twelve months, while domestic matters may keep you busy with extra planning, re-organisation and hard work.*

JANUARY: MAIN TRENDS: **14–15** The present focus on the past and your personal life may be helping you feel more secure, making this a good time for domestic discussion. **16–17** Strike a balance between fulfilling your own needs and your obligations to others, especially in personal relationships. **23–24** A period of domestic reward in which personal indulgence in nostalgia may be of especial meaning. **KEY DATES: HIGHS 8–9** Major plans and schemes may benefit from a little good fortune; push your luck a little! **LOWS 21–22** Don't allow a narrow viewpoint to restrict you, but rein in over-ambitious tendencies.

FEBRUARY: MAIN TRENDS: 1–3 Although you'll enjoy showing off and the more you can do so the happier you'll be, you must beware of too much ego. **8–9** This trend may help you focus and avoid distractions. Getting things done should come with a good deal of satisfaction. **19–20** A harmonious time for personal relationships; your manner is optimistic and this positivity rubs off on those around you. **KEY DATES: HIGHS 4–6** Heed the call and check out any new possibilities during this lucky phase. **LOWS 17–18** Although there may be obstacles to deal with, don't let them overwhelm you.

MARCH: MAIN TRENDS: 5–6 You want to feel intellectually challenged and, interestingly, you may find that everyday routines provide this. Make use of your superior judgement, too. **18–19** Some good advice and help from a friend may enable you to get things done and avoid struggling alone. **20–21** Trends indicate that a matter from the past may re-emerge. Don't let your emotions undermine your confidence or efficiency. **KEY DATES: HIGHS 3–4** Someone may be willing to do you a big favour. Approach the future with confidence. **LOWS 15–16** Something you thought would be easy may prove unexpectedly difficult. Bide your time.

APRIL: MAIN TRENDS: 1–2 Trends enhance your ability to relate to others – you'll be an expert in social relationships, now, skilled in making new acquaintances. **3–4** You'll want the freedom to work unhindered; simply let others know where you stand and remain firm. **19–20** Take the opportunity to travel if it arises and broaden your horizons. **KEY DATES: HIGHS 26–27** Make the most of your current enthusiasm and boundless energy, it may prove advantageous, especially in the workplace. **LOWS 12–13** Keep a low profile and leave major decisions on the shelf for a few days while this planetary low patch is in operation.

MAY: MAIN TRENDS: 8–9 Your chart reveals that new experiences, possibly at work but also perhaps related to health may provide a fresh perspective on things; it may be time to alter some plans. **16–18** The spotlight moves on to communication – an open approach may lead to some magic in personal relationships. **21–22** A financially successful time is indicated; you may be able to enjoy some of the good things of life. **KEY DATES: HIGHS 23–25** A forward moving trend with plenty comings and goings; decide what you want and stick to it. **LOWS 9–10** Minor let-downs or a personal setback may leave you a little insecure. Remember: this, too, will pass.

JUNE: MAIN TRENDS: 4–5 A good time to discuss an idea with others; it may prove fruitful, especially at work. Look for inspiration from places you visit. **17–19** This trend will help you to communicate well with others and make you charming and persuasive! **22–24** Personal activities now centre around family affairs, especially nostalgic ones. Enjoy a trip down memory lane. **KEY DATES: HIGHS 20–21**

Approach problems with faith in yourself and attempt a new approach. A truly open mind opens new doors. **LOWS 5–7** The planets do not favour grandiose new schemes – plan wisely and accept that there may be setbacks.

JULY: MAIN TRENDS: 5–6 There's lots on offer out in the big wide world that interests you. Broaden your horizons, even if it means flying solo for a while. **21–22** A phase of increasing self-confidence and dynamic action. You are proud of yourself, and this puts you in the best of moods. **25–26** This planetary influence indicates that you might want to rethink your life and where it's going, especially if you feel there are obstacles standing in your way. **KEY DATES: HIGHS 17–18** Lady Luck is on your side and this combined with your uncanny ability to spot opportunities suggests a very positive time. **LOWS 3–4; 30–31** Don't rely solely on your own judgment now, ask for help.

AUGUST: MAIN TRENDS: 7–8 Prepare for a satisfying result in business during this fruitful period for some of life's material pleasures. **11–12** Your career ambitions may gather speed, but this may mean shelving a personal plan close to your heart. **21–22** Trends suggest that you will be keeping the people close to you happy and be enjoying harmonious social or romantic relationships now. **KEY DATES: HIGHS 13–15** This monthly high is a good time to take a little, measured chance, especially professionally. **LOWS 26–27** Despite all your best efforts, luck isn't really on your side. Remain calm and ride out the trend.

SEPTEMBER: MAIN TRENDS: 8–9 You may be putting on quite a bold front and happy to show your leadership skills and ambitions. Make sure you channel this into something constructive. **12–13** A hidden matter may come to light; rely on those closest to you to provide the way through. **20–21** Trends indicate a time of retreat, but you should still find fulfilment in personal relationships. Take care not to let someone down. **KEY DATES: HIGHS 10–11** A high-profile period – you feel all-powerful and keen to make new plans. **LOWS 22–24** Take things one at a time at work and avoid any risk-taking.

OCTOBER: MAIN TRENDS: 5–6 Ask your friends for help if you need to find some personal freedom. **15–16** A go-ahead period in your career when you can handle several jobs at once with some success. Important new information may come to light. **23–24** Trends suggest you may feel confused over a personal matter – take care not to be blinded by optimism just because the rosy view of life suits you. **KEY DATES: HIGHS 7–8** A great time for new initiatives; if you have had a plan in mind, now is the time to put it into action. **LOWS 20–21** During the planetary low, keeping life simple and undemanding is the wisest course of action.

NOVEMBER: MAIN TRENDS: 6–7 Some situations outlive their usefulness, and it may now be time to remove any deadwood from your life – something you learn now may confirm that personal change is essential. **11–12** News from outside your personal sphere may raise your spirits. Make plans to get out and socialise or make this a special time for yourself and a partner. **21–22** You may find others interesting, but you yourself have much to offer, especially at a social occasion. **KEY DATES: HIGHS 3–5; 30** Take any opportunity to get out and about and get the most from life. **LOWS 16–17** You may be lacking in energy, so pace yourself carefully.

DECEMBER: MAIN TRENDS: 16–17 You may feel vulnerable about a personal matter. Share your feelings with understanding family members and friends. **21–22** Dynamic and industrious, you should be doing well professionally. Weigh up a small, cautious risk to achieve a short-term goal. **26–27** The aftermath of Christmas may see you craving your own company; unfortunately, though, there may be someone who wants your attention. **KEY DATES: HIGHS 1–2; 28–29** If there's a decision to make, you may have the edge and be able to turn things to your advantage. **LOWS 14–15** You may feel that you aren't getting what you deserve in life; keep calm because it's likely that a change of outlook is all that's needed.

CAPRICORN BORN PEOPLE
Birthdays: 22 December to 20 January inclusive
Planet: Saturn. Birthstone: Garnet. Lucky day: Saturday

Keynote for the Year: *A year when you should enjoy your creative skills. You will be generally in the limelight, though thoughts of taking up serious new studies also has a powerful appeal.*

JANUARY: MAIN TRENDS: 6–7 Be mindful in your approach to life at the start of this year. You should find this helps you give things your undivided attention. **20–21** Under pressure, you're not about to let anything stand in your way – this is just as well, as you should accomplish your goals quickly. **26–27** Don't allow false modesty to get in the way of big ideas. Focus on the main chance and make use of a bit of luck if it comes your way. **KEY DATES: HIGHS 10–11** Favourable influences surround your work and career – make the most of them. **LOWS 23–24** Relax and take things easy, as your energy will deplete all too easily.

FEBRUARY: MAIN TRENDS: 10–11 Work with friends or as part of a team to give you some personal freedom; you might meet someone new and inspirational. **14–15** Your reserves of tact and diplomacy could be stretched to the limit in a work environment. Follow your own individual path when it comes to making progress. **22–23** All that's needed to make life go with a swing is a little positive thinking. Your leadership skills may be required in a personal situation. **KEY DATES: HIGHS 7–8** You will enjoy keeping busy, whether at work or socially. **LOWS 19–21** If you cannot avoid certain obligations, keep to the well-trodden path.

MARCH: MAIN TRENDS: 12–13 Prepare for a challenge in your career and work life; success during this period will depend on your focus and self-discipline. **20–21** The pace of everyday events will be quite swift, but make sure not to move on to the next activity before finishing the last. **22–23** Be prepared to compromise in personal relationships and don't let your stubborn side become a problem. **KEY DATES: HIGHS 5–6** This trend brings you an exciting and winning personality, and the ability to work creatively with new ideas. **LOWS 17–19** Resist feelings of impatience and instead take time out for some meditation and mindfulness.

APRIL: MAIN TRENDS: 5–6 The desire to get ahead could mean you feel compelled to remove old situations that no longer work for you. Make a clean break, if necessary. **20–21** Optimistic and with boundless vitality you should enjoy information seeking and conversation with new people. It could satisfy your curiosity. **23–24** Another non-stop, busy period full of discussions, debates and, possibly, short journeys. Be sure to organise your schedule. **KEY DATES: HIGHS 1–2; 28–30** Resist sitting on the fence over an important move and put bold new ideas to the test. **LOWS 14–15** Take care during this low energy phase.

MAY: MAIN TRENDS: 9–10 All kinds of travel or pursuits which broaden your horizons will be pleasurable. Remember that these horizons can be mental, too. **20–22** A dynamic influence fires you up with ambitious ideas – but pay attention to practical limitations and listen to what those in authority have to say now. **24–25** Trends increase your general popularity and help you attract new people into your life. **KEY DATES: HIGHS 26–27** This is a good time to make yourself known to the right people so be sure to keep up a high profile. **LOWS 11–12** You're likely to encounter obstacles in any plan, and this isn't the best time to push your luck.

JUNE: MAIN TRENDS: 11–12 Colleagues should ensure you are up to date on all the latest developments and goings on – use this information to move ahead. **13–14** A very positive time socially – helping friends and relating to them will make you very popular now. **20–21** Use your unique talents and abilities as well as your imagination and you may find you surprise yourself and impress others. **KEY DATES: HIGHS 22–23** The monthly high brings you the motivation to fulfil your ideas and turn your dreams into reality – go for it! **LOWS 8–9** A time of reflection and contemplation; make this your focus and leave aside material ambitions.

JULY: MAIN TRENDS: 1–3 The ups and downs of everyday life may be a little turbulent, and you may need some help. This is not the best time to go it alone. **13–14** Your home environment should be supportive, rewarding and encouraging. **23–24** Trends suggest you may become involved in cultural activities and will enjoy trying out the new and unusual. Long distance travel is also especially favoured. **KEY DATES: HIGHS 19–20** You'll be on top form in decision making, planning and negotiation. **LOWS 5–6** Limit the time you can spare for others and don't let anyone take advantage of you.

AUGUST: MAIN TRENDS: 4–6 Work takes a turn for the better: lines of communication are open, so conversations with superiors should be fruitful. **22–23** Look for an unexpected opportunity to make new friends or develop an existing relationship. If you make the effort, good things may result. **25–26** Trends move on, and you may now encounter challenges at work. Don't take anything for granted. **KEY DATES: HIGHS 16–17** You may hear encouraging news from a friend. **LOWS 1–2; 28–30** Don't stress over the pace of your progress or be too hard on yourself if things fall flat. Ride out the negative trend.

SEPTEMBER: MAIN TRENDS: 1–2 Social co-operation with others may bring you a good opportunity. A good time to make friends and meet kindred spirits. **15–16** Planetary influences may now lead to a kind of inner tension, where an excess of exuberant energy needs to find a release – find it! **23–24** A good time for planning and organising when you have a realistic view of things and plenty of vision for practical tasks. **KEY DATES: HIGHS 12–13** Your chart reveals that you might get a nice surprise, or a little good luck now. **LOWS 25–26** If you need to rethink or even scrap a current plan of action, accept the situation graciously.

OCTOBER: MAIN TRENDS: 7–8 The material things of this world may be tempting, and you are likely to hold on to them once they're yours. **13–14** A particular situation may require some careful attention, especially in your relationship. Tread carefully. **24–25** The planets make this a real high spot for travel – get out and about, there may be pleasant surprises in store. **KEY DATES: HIGHS 9–11** This is a good time to begin something new – work should run smoothly, and your ideas should be accepted by others. **LOWS 22–23** Minor setbacks may be unavoidable right now so don't try too hard to avoid them – work with them.

NOVEMBER: MAIN TRENDS: 2–3 You're now at your best when you can pursue your goals on your own terms – don't let anyone dictate to you. **22–23** Professional ambitions take priority now as you feel you've no time to waste if you want to get ahead. **27–28** Superiors now look favourably upon you, and you may benefit from their advice. You'll thrive working in a partnership. **KEY DATES: HIGHS 6–7** A progressive attitude may impress someone who could contribute to your success. **LOWS 18–20** Certain situations may no longer work effectively, and there are potential pitfalls around you. Be careful.

DECEMBER: MAIN TRENDS: 5–6 Seek some variety in your life and don't be afraid of change. Get out and meet new faces. **13–14** Trends may bring you a new chance; make the most of it, especially if it involves your personal life. **22–23** The lead-up to Christmas will bring a boost to your energy levels and see you busily involved with a few everyday issues as you try to get your daily life to function better. **KEY DATES: HIGHS 3–4; 30–31** You won't be afraid to show your true self as you strike out for what you need now. **LOWS 16–17** A planetary lull – just be patient with yourself if you feel out of sorts.

AQUARIUS BORN PEOPLE
Birthdays: 21 January to 19 February inclusive
Planets: Saturn, Uranus. Birthstone: Amethyst. Lucky day: Saturday

Keynote for the Year: A great year for putting down new domestic roots, possibly even expanding your home; finance and resources may be another matter, however, requiring a careful approach.

JANUARY: MAIN TRENDS: 15–17 A time when priorities at home and in the family may demand you spend less time at work. Get any unspoken thoughts out into the open. **16–17** A sense of accomplishment is now within your grasp. Develop your own plans to get there. **20–21** Social trends work out nicely and may leave you feeling popular. Catch up on old contacts and work as part of a team. **KEY DATES: HIGHS 12–13** Be open and receptive to new ideas during this potentially lucrative period. **LOWS 25–27** Get some expert advice on a plan and be ready to compromise if you need to.

FEBRUARY: MAIN TRENDS: 1–3 Although motivated and focused on a particular ambition, you tend to do things the hard way, as if trying to prove a point. Don't! Go with the flow. **17–18** You may have to overcome the mental restlessness that this trend brings. A simple change of scenery may be all that is required. **24–26** Trends boost communications, so expect some heart-warming and uplifting news now, most likely from a loved one or trusted friend. **KEY DATES: HIGHS 9–10** The monthly high indicates success and freedom so be bold and free spirited. **LOWS 22–23** Take a break if you can, and delegate some responsibility.

MARCH: MAIN TRENDS: 5–6 You should be making good progress, even if you fall short of your own expectations. Your talent lies in bringing out the best in people. **12–13** A new project may have to be scrapped as ongoing ones need attention. Move on when it's practical to do so. **22–23** A time of social fulfilment, when the atmosphere should be harmonious and a partner or a new friend has a special role to play in your affairs. **KEY DATES: HIGHS 7–8** A good time for your love life; spend quality time with your partner. **LOWS 20–21** Take time to replenish your energy – overdoing it during this period simply won't work.

APRIL: MAIN TRENDS: 6–7 Prepare to meet someone who has a good effect on you. Personal relationships are your strength, and it may be time for a heart to heart with a special someone. **14–15** Your spirits are up and you're in the mood to socialise. Lady Luck may pay you a visit, too! **19–20** There may be new love interest on the horizon. At the very least, you can look forward to a warm reception from others. **KEY DATES: HIGHS 3–4** Someone in your social circle will bring out the best in you. Your relationship should also be strong. **LOWS 16–18** Wind down important tasks during this planetary low patch.

MAY: MAIN TRENDS: 3–5 This influence suggests dynamic action and persuasive skill. You will soon lead others along the path to your ideas. **9–10** You may be in a position of power and influence at work, if only because of your charming but uncompromising manner. **20–21** Look forward to enjoyable and rewarding emotional experiences, especially in your love life. You are very generous with your affection. **KEY DATES: HIGHS 1–2; 28–29** Trends suggest that a general improvement in your finances is in store. **LOWS 13–15** Prepare to be feeling temporarily sluggish and less inclined to go for your ambitions. Get some rest.

JUNE: MAIN TRENDS: 1–2 You may encounter a challenging issue at work and perhaps even some conflict that requires fast action. Co-operate with those in power and authority. **4–5** Money and work are strongly highlighted in your chart; put your ideas to the test and make them work. **26–27** Friends and colleagues gather around to support you now. You may get some crucial input from a friend.

KEY DATES: HIGHS 24–25 You will find something extraordinary in everyday life now and may also learn a valuable lesson. **LOWS 10–11** Trends strongly advise against any risky undertakings now, especially if they relate to money.

JULY: MAIN TRENDS: 4–5 A good time for careful planning and working through your responsibilities – certain material plans ought to be doing rather nicely indeed. **19–20** Emotional situations may be intense, even challenging, but trust your first instincts about others. **25–27** Ambitious ideas and strong desires come to the fore today and can be pursued with energy – but there's still plenty of good advice to be had from colleagues. **KEY DATES: HIGHS 21–23** Make the most of a social invitation – there may be an excellent opportunity to form a new friendship. **LOWS 7–9** Inspiration may sag, and life feel burdensome. Take it easy.

AUGUST: MAIN TRENDS: 6–7 Certain things you have come to depend upon may no longer be quite as supportive as they used to be. You may have to go it alone in some instances. **20–21** It appears that your sense of adventure will be strong right now; you'll be drawn to the new and unusual so follow your heart. **22–23** You may think you give the best advice, but remember, everyone has their own personal style. **KEY DATES: HIGHS 18–19** The best time of this month to make a decision, or to throw your energy into getting what you want. **LOWS 3–5; 31** Focus on tasks that can be completed quickly at these times.

SEPTEMBER: MAIN TRENDS: 2–3 You may feel a strong need to do your own thing and get some variety into your life. Be prepared to experiment with unfamiliar ideas. **22–23** Whether at work or at home you will benefit from being organised now. Look for improvements that will make your life easier. **24–25** Creative activities are positively highlighted, and you may also prove to be the proverbial life and soul of the party. **KEY DATES: HIGHS 14–15** Dynamic and active, be ready to take on whatever life throws you. **LOWS 1; 27–28** Expect to need to work independently, and to feel rewarded by any small victory.

OCTOBER: MAIN TRENDS: 4–5 The way forward now is to keep things simple, although an emotional issue may mean that your judgment is somewhat clouded when it comes to making a decision. **18–19** Make sure to balance out a busy social life with personal obligations if you're to keep things working constructively. **22–23** A good time to spend at home; family relationships give you emotional strength and personal issues may be successfully resolved. **KEY DATES: HIGHS 11–12** Use your excess energy to catch up on things at work. **LOWS 24–26** Wind down any big plans and lie low during the monthly low patch.

NOVEMBER: MAIN TRENDS: 12–13 Trends make you thirsty for a new experience – a change of scenery may help but be open to advice if it is offered. **16–17** The help and advice of friends and colleagues continues to be important and may help you consolidate important matters. **23–24** A plan that's so far been up in the air may now get the green light – it is no coincidence that you seem to get the help you need when you need it. **KEY DATES: HIGHS 8–9** You may need to take a small risk in a personal matter; if necessary, consider striking out on your own. **LOWS 21–22** Prepare for some temporary disappointments now.

DECEMBER: MAIN TRENDS: 7–8 You may be a little socially withdrawn and concerned about important feelings you need to get across to someone – the sooner you do so, the better. **12–13** Get a breath of fresh air and take a break from obligations and duties. Travel is positively highlighted. **20–21** Trends assist you to get the most from life, whether through social gatherings or seeking out new experiences outside your private world. **KEY DATES: HIGHS 5–6** Set out to enjoy the good things of life and you should find you have the knack of finding them. **LOWS 18–19** Check your facts and don't rely on a promise made to you.

PISCES BORN PEOPLE

Birthdays: 20 February to 20 March inclusive
Planets: Jupiter, Neptune. Birthstone: Bloodstone. Lucky day: Thursday

Keynote for the Year: With taskmaster Saturn in your sign, expect various issues to handle – patience and effort will win the day, but also accept some help from friends this year.

JANUARY: MAIN TRENDS: 10–12 Socially, others won't be prepared for your assertive mood and certain forceful views on your part may create the wrong impression. Take care, Pisces. **23–25** Your mind is alert and alive to wider issues in the world. Make the most of your sense of adventure and readiness to try something fresh. **26–27** If there is something you need to jettison from your life, be firm and decided, but there is no need to be ruthless. **KEY DATES: HIGHS 14–15** Build on any recent starts or big new projects and you may be rewarded. **LOWS 28–29** Keep your ambitions on the backburner for a day or so during the monthly low patch.

FEBRUARY: MAIN TRENDS: 8–10 If others try your patience, consider the fact that there are strong emotions in the air, including your own. **12–13** Heeding the old adage, 'look after the small things and the big ones will take care of themselves' will pay dividends in many areas of life, but especially at work. **18–19** A restless time when you may feel the need for freedom and adventure, but you may not be ready to accept extra responsibility. **KEY DATES: HIGHS 11–12** Trends will assist you if you want to break loose and carve out your own path. **LOWS 24–26** With low energy, you approach tasks half-heartedly. Rest if you can.

MARCH: MAIN TRENDS: 7–8 Unexpected changes can disrupt the usual order and routine of your life – but consider if these might not be a blessing in disguise. **17–18** Something from your past or private world is helpful to you now, so helpful that it may clear up a present problem and guide the way forward. **30–31** Planetary influences favour innovative ideas; watch and listen for practical advice at work, especially from someone in your team. **KEY DATES: HIGHS 9–10** Be optimistic and put your faith in the future – it may pay off. **LOWS 22–24** Don't give up on your plans but accept they may have to be shelved for now.

APRIL: MAIN TRENDS: 3–4 You should be productive at work, if only through sheer will and determination. But the planets guide you. **17–18** The planetary focus is mostly on teamwork and co-operation with friends. Your input should be influential. **21–22** Work carefully and methodically towards a worthwhile goal. Certain life choices you're making now may lead to an unexpected, nice surprise. **KEY DATES: HIGHS 5–6** You benefit from your intuition and your enthusiasm for life moves up a notch. A long-held desire may be achieved. **LOWS 19–20** The pull of the past is strong – if this disturbs you, just take one thing at a time.

MAY: MAIN TRENDS: 19–20 Don't get trapped in memories of the past, they will only hold you back. Think plans through clearly and don't become side-tracked. **23–24** In an assertive mood, you may get things done but beware a tendency to lack tact and diplomacy. **28–29** Almost certainly, you will be getting the most from the social and romantic worlds. Your love life should be in particularly good shape. **KEY DATES: HIGHS 3–4** Seize any new or unexpected opportunities to get ahead during the monthly high. **LOWS 16–17** Even the best plans may run into confusion and fall flat. Remember that this phase will soon pass.

JUNE: MAIN TRENDS: 3–4 What happens today culturally or socially may lead to some enlightening experiences. A good influence for taking an overview of things. **15–17** This could be a hectic phase and you have your work cut out keeping life on an even keel. A personal matter may be distracting and require attention. **21–22** A great time for personal relationships when your partner should be loving and supportive. **KEY DATES: HIGHS 26–27** Any pioneering venture will appeal to you now, especially if it offers scope to broaden your horizons. **LOWS 12–14** Prepare for a few practical setbacks and temporary delays.

JULY: MAIN TRENDS: 1–2 An intellectual peak when you may score some points with the power of your personality. Some of your proposals may find a sympathetic ear. **22–23** Cultural and intellectual pursuits continue to interest you. If you get the chance to meet new people from other cultures, take it. **28–29** Potentially a satisfying period for your money – acquiring, saving or spending. **KEY DATES: HIGHS 24–25** Your biggest professional asset now is your gift for communication – use it wisely. **LOWS 10–11** Don't expect miracles in anything you are working on. A short hiatus looks likely.

AUGUST: MAIN TRENDS: 1–2 Your finances look to be stable now – don't put this situation at risk. **8–9** You may have reason to question if someone is leading you up the garden path. Take life easy and don't become obsessed by a particular issue. **27–28** Although trends suggest something may pique your curiosity, don't become distracted by trivialities. Emotional relationships should be comforting. **KEY DATES: HIGHS 20–21** Most of the pieces in your life are in good shape and now you may be able to improve them further. **LOWS 6–7** An emotional issue may put you under pressure – the wise thing is to accept things and go with the flow.

SEPTEMBER: MAIN TRENDS: 9–10 Trends suggest that some relationships may need change. Let these changes happen. **14–15** You may find yourself in disagreement with someone over a practical issue at work – be calm and tactful. **23–24** Your own ego is likely to help you get your own way with others, especially in your relationship. **KEY DATES: HIGHS 16–17** The monthly high will see you ready to push on with plans and initiatives, especially those that may be lucrative. **LOWS 2–4; 29–30** Go easy on yourself, and others, and accept that you may have to wait your turn for something.

OCTOBER: MAIN TRENDS: 3–4 Make an early start and concentrate hard at work but beware of getting on the wrong side of superiors. **21–22** Don't put off dealing with something, whether personal or professional, because you're afraid of the outcome – stop worrying and press on. **23–25** Influences bring out the homebird in you, and your attention turns to the domestic scene. Let the rest of the world go by. **KEY DATES: HIGHS 14–15** Trends favour a small flutter now but be sure you only gamble what you can afford to lose. **LOWS 1; 27–28** Keep your expectations of others simple – they may be less able to help for very good reasons.

NOVEMBER: MAIN TRENDS: 3–5 You should enjoy cultural interests and philosophical discussions with friends. Travel is also favoured. **15–16** Use common sense and reason at work, or you risk falling foul of someone in authority. **25–26** The sheer force of your personality helps you get what you want. Focus on creative ventures or just being out and about, getting your message across. **KEY DATES: HIGHS 10–11** Something that had been at the drawing board stage should now get up and running. **LOWS 23–24** There may be plenty to try your patience now, but this doesn't mean you should over-react. Remain calm.

DECEMBER: MAIN TRENDS: 1–3 The tempo of life may quicken just a few paces, but don't let this turn into a crisis because you're trying to do too much. Focus on your real priorities. **10–11** A successful period when you should find it easy to achieve your goals. Trends suggest you'll be especially efficient while working alongside others. **18–19** Look out for some help with money or finances. You may find the right person at the right moment if you look for them. **KEY DATES: HIGHS 7–9** A great time to start a new project – your optimistic attitude could open doors. **LOWS 20–22** Certain responsibilities may require a practical approach that you feel you are lacking. Bide your time.

Racing with the Jockeys in 2024

ASTROLOGICAL POINTERS TO POSSIBLE WINNING PERIODS

The astrologically compiled dates below are presented to race-goers in the hope that they will point the way to some successful winning periods during the 2024 racing season. Specially recommended = sr.

FAVOURABLE PERIODS FOR FLAT-RACE JOCKEYS

D. PROBERT: Born 1 January 1988. Should do best in the summer months at meetings in the south this year. His favourable periods are: 27 March; 2–3, 6, 13, 15, 23–28 April (15 sr); 1, 7, 14–18, 24–27, 31 May (1, 18 sr); 3–6, 10, 16–17, 22–28 June (3, 16 sr); 2–5, 17, 21, 27–30 July (2–5 sr); 2, 7, 10–13, 16, 24, 31 August (16 sr); 3–4, 7–10, 14, 19–25, 30 September (4, 25 sr); 1–3, 9, 11–13, 16, 22–24, 30 October (11–13 sr); 3–4, 8 November.

H. DOYLE: Born 11 October 1996. Likely to succeed best on two-year-olds in mid-season. Her favourable periods are: 24–27 March; 5–8, 13–17, 24–26 April; 2–6, 10, 17–23, 30 May (30 sr); 7–11, 16, 21–24, 30 June; 1, 4, 13–18, 22–23 July (13–18 sr); 3–4, 12–13, 17–26, 31 August (31 sr); 4, 13–17, 23, 27 September (27 sr); 3, 6, 12, 17, 21–23, 27 October (3, 23 sr); 1, 7–8 November.

W. BUICK: Born 22 July 1988. Southern venues are to be favoured, particularly when it comes to sprinters this year. His favourable periods are: 3–16, 20–22, 24 March; 6, 14–20, 25–30 April (20, 25 sr); 2–6, 10–11, 27 May (2–6, 10–11 sr); 3, 7, 14–17, 22–28 June; 1, 8, 16, 22–23 July (1, 8, 22 sr); 1–3, 6–7, 17–24, 26, 31 August (17, 26 sr); 2, 11, 14–16, 26 September (11 sr); 2, 5, 13, 20–23, 30 October (20 sr); 1–4, 13–17, 27–30 November (1–4 sr).

T. MARQUAND: Born 30 March 1998. Later in the season, sprint handicappers may give the best results. His favourable periods are: 13–14, 21, 26–27 March (27 sr); 2, 10, 13–16, 21–23, 25–28 April (23 sr); 3, 8, 17–23, 31 May (8 sr); 7–10, 12, 21–23 June; 2–6, 11–13, 22, 27 July (12 sr); 4, 6, 11–12, 24–25 August (11, sr); 1–3, 6–11, 14–17, 25–29 September (14–17 sr); 8–11, 16–17, 26–27 October (16 sr); 1–5 November.

FAVOURABLE PERIODS FOR NATIONAL HUNT JOCKEYS

H. SKELTON: Born 20 September 1989. Should excel navigating hurdles at northern venues this year. His favourable periods are: 23–26 January (23 sr); 3–6, 13–14, 21–23, 26 February; 6–10, 15–16, 21–22, 30 March (15–16 sr); 4–6, 8, 16, 25, 29–30 April (29–30 sr); 6–14, 24–26 May (26 sr); 14–16, 22–25 June; 26–31 July; 10–15, 22–27 August; 1–3, 17–18 September (3 sr); 6–12, 16, 25–27, 31 October (16 sr); 1–3, 16, 21, 24–26 November (24 sr); 5–8, 10, 22 December.

B. HUGHES: Born 27 June 1985. Likely to have best results in chases on shorter courses in the north. His favourable periods are: 1–3, 9, 16–21, 23–26 January (26 sr); 2, 8–10, 13–16, 23–25 February (25 sr); 6–10, 12–15, 26 March (15 sr); 3–5, 16, 21–25, 29 April (3–5 sr); 3, 6, 8, 11–16, 25–28 May; 3–7, 18–23, 28–29 June; 7–10, 14–21 July; 2, 28, 31 August; 3–5, 13–15, 25–28 September; 6–8, 10, 24 October; 9–11, 28–30 November; 1, 9, 18 December (18 sr).

S. TWISTON-DAVIES: Born 15 October 1992. In the second half of the year, chases in the south may see most wins. His favourable periods are: 5–6, 14–16, 21–23 January; 1, 5–6, 13–14, 25 February (25 sr); 5–6, 8–11, 21–23, 30 March (21 sr); 1–3, 13–18, 23, 30 April (13–16 sr); 3–5, 11–15, 21–25 May (11 sr); 1–3, 17–22, 30 June; 1–5, 23–29 July; 5–9, 14–21, 26 August; 4–11, 20–23, 30 September (23 sr); 12–16, 21–26 October (26 sr); 1–2, 19–20, 26 November; 1, 5–6, 12, 24 December (5 sr).

AMAZING HORSE RACING SYSTEM

PROFIT OVER 10 YEARS £292,850

AVERAGE YEARLY GAIN £27,500 TO £50 SINGLES

PLUS ★ PLUS ★ PLUS

HORSE RACING INFORMATION

BIG BUZZ SATURDAY SUPER YANKEE

PROFIT LAST 3 YEARS £156,395 TO £2 STAKE

FREE ★ FREE ★ FREE

JOIN OUR SYNDICATE - WON 20-1 WON 25-1 WON 33-1

FIRST TIP FREE

WRITE OR PHONE (est. 34 YEARS) **02392 521873 – 0843 850 1306**

MR Q. 140 ST VINCENT ROAD, GOSPORT, HAMPSHIRE PO12 4RF

Raphael's Astronomical Ephemeris 2024

The most reliable astronomical ephemeris you can buy. Available from good bookshops, phone 01256 302699 or from www.foulsham.com

Also available in two Multi-Year Collections

1950–2000	2000–2050
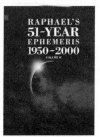	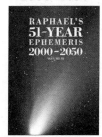
978-0-572-03908-0	978-0-572-03909-7

978-0-572-04836-5

Racing with the Trainers in 2024

ASTROLOGICAL POINTERS TO POSSIBLE WINNING PERIODS

The astrologically compiled dates below are presented to race-goers in the hope that they will point the way to some successful winning periods during the 2024 racing season. Specially recommended = sr

FAVOURABLE PERIODS FOR FLAT-RACE TRAINERS

A. M. BALDING: Born 29 December 1972. Ought to see his best moments with fillies during most of this season. His favourable periods are: 24 March; 10, 12–17, 22–28 April (12 sr); 3–6, 12–14, 22–24 May (14 sr); 2–5, 13, 20, 22–29 June (22–29 sr); 1, 4, 14–17, 25–28 July (25–28 sr); 2–3, 11–15, 25–31 August; 5, 13–15, 21, 27–29 September (29 sr); 6–7, 11, 19, 22–27, 31 October (22–27 sr); 1, 8–10 November.

C. JOHNSTON: Born 4 October 1990. Likely to succeed best with three-year-olds in northern handicaps this year. His favourable periods are: 10, 27–29 March; 7–11, 13–17, 24–25 April; 2–5, 9, 17–23, 27 May (27 sr); 7–11, 14, 21–24, 30 June; 4, 7–8, 14–20, 24–26 July; 1, 14–16, 26–29 August; 6–7, 11, 13–15, 30 September (11 sr); 3–5, 9–10, 15–18, 28 October (9–10 sr); 4, 7–10, 13–17, 22–24 November (22–24 sr).

J. GOSDEN: Born 30 March 1951. Likely to excel mid-season at races in the midlands with two-year-olds. His favourable periods are: 17, 29–30 March; 2–4, 7–9, 17, 27, 29–30 April (29–30 sr); 10–11, 16, 23–27, 31 May (10–11 sr); 4–9, 11–14, 21, 26 June (11–14 sr); 1, 3–4, 11, 17, 22–24 July (17 sr); 2–6, 14, 20–23 August; 1, 3–4, 7, 13–14, 21, 27, 30 September (21 sr); 1–2, 14–18, 22–24, 30 October; 1, 3, 14–16, 24–29 November.

FAVOURABLE PERIODS FOR NATIONAL HUNT TRAINERS

P. F. NICHOLLS: Born 17 April 1962. Should do especially well with two-year-olds, especially in the last third of this year. His favourable periods are: 4–6, 22–27, 31 January (22–27 sr); 1, 6–10, 22–26 February (22 sr); 11–14, 19, 20–24 March; 19–22, 29 April; 2–3, 10–12, 28–31 May (10–12 sr); 1–4, 9–10, 22–23 June (9–10 sr); 6–9, 16–19, 22–30 July (16–19 sr); 1–3, 6–9, 11–16, 24–26 August; 2–3, 16–19, 22–23 September; 10–14, 19, 22–24, 31 October (14 sr); 3–6, 10, 14–16, 23–27 November (10 sr); 3–9, 19, 21 December (19 sr).

N. HENDERSON: Born 10 December 1950. Northern meetings ought to provide his most triumphant moments, especially in the first half of the year. His favourable periods are: 2–3, 9–14, 20–22, 25–29 January; 1, 15, 20–24 February; 2–4, 7–10, 14, 21–22, 28–29 March; 1–2, 7, 13–14, 19–20, 27 April; 2–4, 6–7, 11, 29 May; 2–4, 14–17, 22, 29 June; 4–6, 19–20, 27–28 July; 1–5, 8–10, 26, 29 August (1–2, 26 sr); 1, 7–8, 28–31 October; 4–5, 9, 24 November; 18, 21, 25–29 December (29 sr).

D. McCAIN Jnr: Born 13 June 1960. Should succeed with his three- and four-year-olds in the south this year. His favourable periods are: 19–20, 26–31 January (19, 26 sr); 2–4, 11–13, 20–24 February (2–4, 13 sr); 2–3, 14–16, 20–22, 29–31 March; 2–3, 6–8, 25 April; 1–3, 16–22, 29–30 May (16 sr); 12–14, 18, 26–27 June (26–27 sr); 4, 9, 10–13, 19–20, 24–26 July; 2, 9, 14–17, 28–29 August; 11–12, 18, 23, 26 October (26 sr); 1–3, 10–14, 21–29 November; 2–4, 10, 26–29 December.

Greyhound Racing Numbers for 2024

TRAP-NUMBER FORECASTS FOR POTENTIAL SUCCESS

Each area of the UK has a ruling planetary number, and each month of 2024 has a prominent fortunate planetary number. This forecast is based on a combination of those numbers to provide a list of the most propitious dates for betting and the trap numbers most likely to be successful.

The table gives the main areas of the UK and under each monthly heading, the first column shows the best dates for betting, and the second, shaded column gives the trap numbers for the winner and the second dog.

Whilst making no claim to infallibility, this forecast should offer those who enjoy an occasional jaunt to greyhound race meetings a way of aligning their activities with the best planetary influences and potentially increasing their success rate.

MEETING	JAN	FEB	MAR	APRIL	MAY	JUNE	JULY	AUG	SEPT	OCT	NOV	DEC
London	6–10 (2 5)	3–10 (1 5)	1–11 (3 5)	1–5 (3 4)	3–8 (2 4)	10–14 (1 3)	5–10 (4 5)	12–15 (1 2)	2–8 (4 5)	1–7 (2 5)	3–10 (1 4)	2–6 (3 5)
	22–27 (2 3)	15–20 (1 3)	16–25 (1 2)	16–22 (3 6)	23–30 (4 5)	23–28 (3 5)	20–28 (1 3)	23–28 (3 4)	21–27 (1 2)	27–31 (1 3)	23–26 (2 5)	19–24 (3 4)
Birmingham	1–8 (4 6)	1–10 (1 3)	4–11 (3 5)	7–14 (1 6)	1–6 (2 3)	7–12 (1 3)	9–13 (3 5)	6–14 (1 2)	3–10 (1 5)	2–8 (3 5)	5–11 (2 4)	9–13 (2 6)
	19–24 (1 2)	22–25 (3 4)	19–24 (2 6)	23–28 (2 5)	22–27 (3 4)	21–24 (2 3)	25–29 (4 6)	24–28 (2 4)	26–30 (3 4)	22–25 (1 3)	21–27 (2 5)	26–31 (1 5)
Manchester	1–6 (2 3)	8–14 (1 4)	2–5 (3 6)	1–4 (2 4)	2–8 (1 5)	8–13 (2 4)	1–5 (2 5)	9–12 (5 6)	8–15 (3 5)	10–13 (1 5)	3–6 (2 5)	1–8 (2 3)
	21–25 (3 6)	22–24 (1 3)	21–28 (2 4)	27–30 (2 4)	23–26 (3 6)	22–29 (4 5)	22–26 (2 4)	21–25 (2 3)	20–25 (4 5)	24–28 (1 6)	19–24 (1 3)	15–20 (2 5)
Newcastle	4–11 (1 4)	2–5 (2 4)	4–10 (1 2)	7–14 (1 5)	1–7 (2 4)	9–11 (4 6)	1–4 (1 3)	2–8 (1 4)	3–8 (4 6)	5–10 (2 3)	4–9 (2 6)	8–12 (3 5)
	25–29 (1 4)	22–25 (1 2)	21–28 (2 5)	22–27 (2 6)	22–31 (1 5)	20–24 (2 6)	28–31 (2 4)	21–29 (1 3)	27–30 (3 6)	21–26 (1 2)	22–27 (3 6)	23–27 (1 5)
Sheffield	4–10 (2 5)	2–7 (1 4)	5–12 (3 5)	5–11 (2 6)	2–9 (4 5)	2–8 (2 3)	5–8 (2 5)	6–12 (1 6)	2–5 (1 4)	2–7 (5 6)	5–13 (2 3)	7–10 (2 3)
	22–27 (2 4)	18–26 (1 6)	22–25 (3 4)	25–30 (5 6)	21–28 (4 6)	25–30 (1 4)	25–30 (1 2)	24–31 (1 5)	23–28 (2 4)	22–29 (3 4)	24–29 (1 5)	26–31 (4 6)
Wales	9–12 (1 3)	5–9 (5 6)	1–6 (3 4)	2–10 (2 5)	4–8 (2 3)	5–10 (3 6)	1–8 (2 3)	1–7 (2 5)	10–13 (1 4)	2–9 (2 5)	9–12 (2 3)	2–6 (3 4)
	15–22 (3 5)	23–28 (1 4)	4–10 (2 6)	24–29 (2 5)	21–28 (3 4)	19–24 (2 3)	21–27 (1 3)	21–24 (5 6)	22–27 (3 4)	24–31 (3 5)	20–26 (1 5)	18–24 (2 6)
South of England	1–6 (1 3)	4–10 (1 2)	3–9 (5 6)	8–13 (1 3)	2–4 (1 5)	6–13 (4 6)	3–11 (3 5)	2–9 (1 5)	8–12 (3 6)	9–14 (1 2)	3–7 (1 3)	10–14 (4 5)
	21–28 (2 4)	19–25 (1 4)	15–22 (2 3)	22–26 (3 5)	24–31 (1 3)	24–30 (2 4)	21–26 (2 4)	28–31 (1 2)	20–26 (2 3)	25–31 (5 6)	22–28 (3 5)	22–27 (3 4)

Psychic Readings

To get a general psychic reading.
Call 020 8748 2720
£20.00 to D. Stevens.

The Free Spirits Club

Friends, pen pals, romance.
UK-Wide. No Internet needed.
Call for details: **01633 526523**

Old Moore's Almanack

is published each year in June
and is available from all good newsagents
and booksellers.

You can also obtain a copy from Foulsham,
*The Old Barrel Store, Drayman's Lane,
Marlow, Bucks SL7 2FF* (01628 400600).
You can also buy online at
www.foulsham.com or phone 01256 302699.

Who was Old Moore?

Francis Moore, a Shropshire lad, was born in Bridgnorth in 1657, into poverty. Despite his humble beginnings he taught himself to read and write and developed an interest in medicine, which at the time was heavily dependent on astrology.

Realising that Bridgnorth offered insufficient scope for his talent he made his way to London, like Dick Whittington, to make his fortune. Providence gave him the chance of studying with the eminent astrologer John Partridge, who was popular with London's high society. Having added medical astrology to his skills, Dr Francis Moore set up his own business in Southwark. Good at his profession, he was privileged to attain the status of Physician to the Court of King Charles II.

Moore launched his first black and white broadsheet in 1697 in support of his Southwark-based apothecary practice – an early advertising campaign! Astrology, combined with his medical advice, was very much in vogue at that time and herbal sales in London shot up. By 1700, with his Court connections, he had compiled the first of his famous *Vox Stellarum* series – *The Voice of the Stars*. The predictions were probably a spin off from his astrological calculations and were included to increase the Almanack sales to a more broadly based public. For those unable to read, special symbols were printed alongside certain days to indicate the importance of the event.

When he died in 1715 Moore's Almanack was taken over by the Worshipful Company of Liveried Stationers who continued to publish it until 1911 when the House of Foulsham bought the copyright. It has been published *every* year since 1697, earning it a place in the *Guinness Book of Records*.

Today a team of astrologers represent Old Moore working 18 months ahead of actual events. They are among the very best and most skilled of UK astrologers. In the Almanack each year Old Moore brings astrological insight into a broad range of editorial features, covering varied subjects from racing to gardening to angling – and not forgetting, of course, the monthly horoscope for each zodiac sign. Why should there be such interest in this simple little book of astrological data and writing? It's down to successful prediction. In the Leader and political editorial which forms the heart of the book, year after year the astrologers describe the direction that the UK and the world will take and generally cover the key players who will take a major role. People keep reading because Old Moore's record is so good they can still use him for their forward planning!

Old Moore predicts modern world affairs with a huge head start. With his historic data records he knows where to look first. There isn't another seer in the world that can claim the duration of accuracy that is published under the by-line Dr Francis Moore.

Best Sowing And Planting Times for the Garden in 2024

WHEN TO PLANT OR SOW BY THE MOON TO GET THE BEST RESULTS

Peas, beans, flowering vegetables and plants which produce fruit above the ground should always be sown under a waxing Moon (the period from New Moon to Full). Potatoes and root crops should always be sown when the Moon is low and below the Earth. If you sow, plant or re-pot at the times set out below, it is reasonably certain you will have really fine results. The times are Greenwich Mean Time. Allowances must be made for British Summer Time.

Month	Day	Planting Times		
JANUARY	10, 11, 12	8.20 to 10.00 am	1.00 to 2.20 pm	
	24, 25, 26	8.05 to 11.35 am	12.50 to 2.40 pm	
FEBRUARY	8, 9, 10	9.10 to 11.00 am	12.30 to 3.05 pm	
	23, 24, 25	8.55 to 11.35 am	12.55 to 3.45 pm	
	Begin sowing legumes, leaf vegetables and root vegetables. Delay beetroot until the weather is mild. Cut early kidney potatoes for seed and use a heater or heat mats to get them started.			
MARCH	9, 10, 11	8.55 am to 12.55 pm	1.15 to 2.20 pm	3.10 to 4.55 pm
	24, 25, 26	8.45 am to 12.15 pm	1.10 to 2.40 pm	3.15 to 4.15pm
	Planting and sowing into the ground can begin this month. Sow asparagus, celery, brassicas, and continue with root vegetables and legumes. Cabbages, onion sets and sea-kale may be planted out.			
APRIL	7, 8, 9	7.15 to 11.10 am	1.15 to 2.15 pm	4.15 to 5.10 pm
	22, 23, 24	7.35 to 11.15 am	12.10 to 2.10 pm	3.40 to 5.05 pm
	Sowing of tomatoes and peppers can begin indoors. Continue sowing legumes, brassicas and leaf vegetables for the main summer crop. Plant out rhubarb, artichokes, asparagus and small salad vegetables. Tie up lettuce and in dry weather water seed in beds.			
MAY	7, 8, 9	7.55 to 11.55 am	12.40 to 3.15 pm	4.15 to 6.50 pm
	22, 23, 24	8.50 to 12.50 pm	1.50 to 2.25 pm	3.55 to 6.15 pm
	Sow cucumber, dwarf bean, runner beans and a full crop of kidney beans. Transplant cabbage, winter greens, cauliflower and celery seedlings. Hoe and stake peas, water newly planted crops.			
JUNE	6, 7, 8	7.25 to 11.50 am	1.10 to 2.25 pm	4.50 to 5.20 pm
	21, 22, 23	7.45 to 11.00 am	12.45 to 2.55 pm	4.40 to 6.35 pm
	Top beans and peas to assist the filling of the pods. Set kidney beans. Thin out onions, leeks, parsnips and early turnips. Plant tomatoes and peppers outdoors. Water all crops well during dry spells.			
JULY	4, 5, 6	6.50 to 11.50 am	1.55 to 3.30 pm	4.10 to 6.35 pm
	20, 21, 22	7.55 to 11.15 am	12.40 to 3.10 pm	4.20 to 7.35 pm
	Plant out the last of the brassicas and cabbages and earth up celery. Lift full-grown winter onions and new potatoes. Pick vine crops as they ripen to encourage new fruit.			
AUGUST	3, 4, 5	6.55 to 10.50 am	12.35 to 2.50 pm	6.50 to 8.50 pm
	18, 19, 20	7.50 to 10.40 am	12.25 to 2.45 pm	6.35 to 8.15 pm
	Sow early cabbages and parsley for the succeeding year, also spinach, broccoli and cauliflower to stand the winter and transplant seedlings. Continue to pick legumes and vine crops as they ripen.			
SEPTEMBER	2, 3, 4	7.50 to 11.10 am	12.40 to 4.10 pm	5.55 to 7.50 pm
	17, 18, 19	7.15 to 11.45 am	1.55 to 3.45 pm	5.35 to 7.20 pm
	Plant some radishes, early cabbages, cauliflower, and some herbs like mint, thyme and tarragon in frames for winter use. Sow the last winter lettuce. Harvest crops before any risk of frost.			
OCTOBER	1, 2, 3	8.55 am to 12.55 pm	1.55 to 3.30 pm	4.40 to 6.35 pm
	16, 17, 18, 31	8.55 to 11.10 am	12.55 to 3.40 pm	4.25 to 5.35 pm
	Plant some radishes, early cabbages, cauliflower, and some herbs like mint, thyme and tarragon in frames for winter use. Sow the last winter lettuce. Harvest crops before any risk of frost.			
NOVEMBER	1, 2, 3	8.25 am to 12.30 pm	2.50 to 4.25 pm	
	14, 15, 16, 30	8.35 am to 12.25 pm	2.30 to 4.15 pm	
	Dig ground once crops are carried off and there is no intention to plant again until spring. Shallots are readily propagated by offcuts. Clear fallen leaves quickly and dispose of diseased plants.			
DECEMBER	1, 2, 3	9.15 am to 1.35 pm	2.35 to 3.15 pm	
	14, 15, 16	9.45 to 10.50 am	1.35 to 3.00 pm	
	29, 30, 31	9.20 am to 1.00 pm	1.25 to 3.40 pm	
	Earth up celery. Sow small salad vegetables in warm borders covered with mats.			

Football Pools Forecast for 2024

This forecast, based on a combination of planetary indications and team colours, lists the teams likely to draw on the dates given, or within two days either side. No claims to infallibility are made and readers should use their own judgement, but forecasts may help them in the final selection.

6 January
Birmingham, Wolves, Fulham, Blackpool, Salford, Wigan

13 January
Ipswich, Reading, Newcastle, Aston Villa, Liverpool

20 January
West Ham, QPR, Charlton Athletic, Dundee

27 January
West Ham, Everton, Watford, West Brom, Bristol City, Sunderland

3 February
Bolton, Rotherham, Wolves, West Ham, Crystal Palace, Preston

10 February
Leicester City, Middlesbrough, Newcastle, Stoke, Reading

17 February
Dundee, Bolton, Wolves, Huddersfield, Manchester City

26 February
Hull City, Sunderland, Oldham, Manchester Utd, Celtic, Blackpool

2 March
Hibernian, Southampton, Crystal Palace, Port Vale, Celtic

9 March
Crystal Palace, Hull City, Ipswich, QPR, Blackpool

16 March
Brentford, West Ham, Arsenal, Exeter, Peterborough, Aston Villa

23 March
Sunderland, Middlesbrough, Crystal Palace, Blackburn

30 March
Chesterfield, Hull City, Rangers, Peterborough, Burnley

6 April
Watford, Brentford, Coventry City, Bolton

13 April
Middlesbrough, Chelsea, Swansea City, Blackpool, Wolves

20 April
Arsenal, Birmingham, Falkirk, Bournemouth, Doncaster, Southampton

27 April
Norwich City, Wigan, QPR, Blackburn, Charlton Athletic, Sunderland, Inverness

4 May
Stoke City, Portsmouth, Torquay Utd, QPR, Reading, Man City

11 May
West Brom, Arsenal, Liverpool, Scunthorpe, Everton, Southampton

18 May
Sunderland, West Ham, Aberdeen, Hibernian, Swansea City, Crystal P

10 August
Bournemouth, Doncaster, Man Utd, Barnsley, Peterborough

17 August
Bradford, Tottenham Hotspur, Norwich City, Burnley

24 August
Man United, Ipswich, Aston Villa, Hull, Southampton, Sheffield Utd

31 August
Chelsea, Crystal Palace, Birmingham, Plymouth, Liverpool

7 September
Arsenal, Charlton Athletic, Preston, Birmingham, Blackburn

14 September
QPR, Birmingham, Bolton, Leeds, Peterborough, Bradford

21 September
Leeds, Coventry, Manchester City, Brighton, Wigan, West Ham

28 September
Manchester Utd, Stoke City, Bristol City, Wolves, Aston Villa, Liverpool

5 October
Celtic, Aberdeen, Wolves, Motherwell, Man Utd, Swansea

12 October
Celtic, Everton, Ipswich, Blackburn, Watford, Brentford, West Ham

19 October
Manchester City, Burnley, Rotherham, Hearts, West Bromwich Albion

26 October
Arsenal, Fulham, Newcastle, Blackburn, Chesterfield, Manchester City, Blackpool

2 November
Dundee Utd, Birmingham, Aston Villa, Bolton, QPR, Chelsea

9 November
Carlisle Utd, Wigan, Hull, Wolves, Fulham, Preston, Barnsley, Everton

16 November
Manchester Utd, Watford, Hearts, Wigan, Preston, Norwich

23 November
Liverpool, West Ham, Reading, Swindon, Bolton

30 November
Arsenal, West Bromwich Albion, Blackpool, Fulham, Swansea City

7 December
Burnley, Middlesbrough, Southampton Town, Reading, Manchester City

14 December
Man City, Bournemouth, Bristol Rovers, Arsenal, Southampton

21 December
Swansea City, Leicester, Blackpool, Chelsea, Bristol City, Reading, Leeds

28 December
Burnley, West Ham, Middlesbrough, Newcastle, Stoke

Angler's Guide for 2024

THE BEST DATES AND TECHNIQUES FOR SUCCESSFUL FISHING

JANUARY: Sport can be hard due to low temperatures, so stick to deeper water on rivers and lakes. Backwaters are a good bet when main rivers are flooded: try float or leger tactics in slack water swims. Shoaling cod may be caught from the beaches, especially in Scotland, on casting gear but they will soon thin out as temperatures rise. **Best days:** 2, 6, 8 (am), 14, 16 (pm), 21, 23 (am), 30, 31 (pm).

FEBRUARY: Predator fishing offers the best action with pike, perch and zander all possible on fish baits, but scale down your tackle if the temperature plummets. Big chub can also be had on leger tactics. Spring salmon on the cards for some anglers, but beach rods will have to work harder for their catches. Flatties will still feature, although bigger fish can be had when afloat. **Best days:** 1, 4, 5 (pm), 8, 9 (am), 11, 14, 17 (am), 19, 20, 22, 24, 26 (pm).

MARCH: The freshwater river season closes this month, but almost all commercial still waters will stay open. If mild weather comes early, head for sheltered lakes which can produce superb mixed catches of roach, bream, carp and even tench. Trout anglers head for deep, still waters from the 15th. **Best days:** 9, 11 (pm), 12, 13, 14 (am), 18, 19, 20 (pm), 21, 22, 25 (am).

APRIL: Beach anglers can enjoy the spring run of codling, while those fishing wrecks can expect bumper hauls of pollack, ling and occasional big cod on artificial baits. Ray fishing good, especially in the Solent. Most flies will take trout on still waters but a more careful approach is needed in rivers. **Best days:** 1, 2, 7, 8 (pm), 10, 13 (am), 16, 17, 18 (pm), 19, 20 (am), 24, 29 (pm).

MAY: Crab baits worthy for early school bass, flounder and eel, while ragworm and lugworm will take their fair share of plaice in harbours and estuaries. Still-water trout should respond to warmer weather and can be taken on floating lines. Carp will be the bulk of catches for commercial still-water anglers. **Best days:** 2, 9, 12 (am), 17 (pm), 23, 24 (am), 27, 28 (pm), 30, 31 (pm).

JUNE: The Glorious 16th will enable specimen tench, carp and bream to be targeted with big baits on both float and leger tackle. Rivers with more pace should provide excellent catches of roach and chub. Beach anglers will find bass more widespread, while their boat counterparts can expect mackerel – the perfect bait for shark and tope – which will start to show off many southern and Welsh ports. **Best days:** 2, 7, 8 (pm), 11, 13 (pm), 14, 16, 17 (am), 19, 20, 21 (pm), 30 (am).

JULY: Top sport on rivers and lakes with virtually all species responsive, mostly to particle baits such as corn, hemp and tares. Try swims with plenty of flow as fish, particularly barbel and bream, will be hungry for oxygen-rich water during hot weather. Evening sessions ideal for fly anglers pursuing trout. Shy mullet may be tempted during quiet days around harbours, and bass will be bigger. **Best days:** 1, 2, 4, 6 (am), 13, 14, 16 (pm), 21, 22, 23, 31 (am).

AUGUST. Low oxygen levels suggest fishing either very early morning or evening periods. Sea anglers afloat can look forward to a multitude of species including bream, bass, pollack, conger and gurnard. Fresh fish baits and crab will outscore all others. **Best days:** 1, 2, 6 (pm), 7, 9 (am), 15, 16 (pm), 20, 23, 26, 29 (am).

SEPTEMBER: Fish will have had time to feed well and big specimens can be expected. Barbel, roach, bream, tench and chub will all be at their optimum weight. Trout anglers may struggle to locate decent fish, although beach and boat fishing will be hunting big bass with sand eel baits, crab or lures. **Best days:** 3, 4, 8, 9 (am), 10, 11, 15, 16 (pm), 20, 21, 22 (am), 26, 27, 28 (am).

OCTOBER: Cooler temperatures may mean slow sport on lakes, but rivers will be at their peak for roach, chub and dace on caster or maggot. Float tactics are good but don't discount leger or feeder gear. Beach anglers expect the first of the winter codling, where lugworm and squid will be top baits. Extra water may prompt decent catches of salmon for game anglers. **Best days:** 1, 4, 5 (am), 8, 9 (pm), 10, 11, 13, 18 (am), 20, 21, 26 (pm).

NOVEMBER: With shorter days, codling will come closer inshore, especially at deeper venues such as steep beaches, harbour walls and piers. Bad weather may mean slower sport for coarse anglers, who need to scale down hooks and baits. Predator hunters can expect big pike on baits rather than lures. **Best days:** 1, 5, 6, 11 (am), 14, 15, 16 (pm), 22, 23 (am), 25, 26, 30 (pm).

DECEMBER: A roving approach is best during colder weather. Try different swims on backwaters, where roach will take bread flake, and chub can be had on cheese paste, bread, worms and cockles. Pin baits hard to the bottom or let them roll in the flow. After a storm is ideal for targeting codling on beaches, when they attack food stirred up by rough weather. Try night sessions for greater success. **Best days:** 7, 8 (am), 10, 11, 14 (pm), 16, 17, 20 (am), 29 (am).

65

Lucky Dates to Play Bingo in 2024

CHECK YOUR ZODIAC SIGN FOR YOUR GOOD-LUCK TIMES

Aries (Birthdays 21 March to 20 April)
4 February to 11 March, 19 June to 30 August, 18 October to 19 November

❀

Taurus (Birthdays 21 April to 21 May)
11 February to 11 April, 4 July to 9 September, 9 November to 19 December

❀

Gemini (Birthdays 22 May to 21 June)
3 January to 24 February, 4 May to 11 July, 3 October to 7 December

❀

Cancer (Birthdays 22 June to 22 July)
29 January to 22 March, 26 June to 4 August, 29 October to 25 December

❀

Leo (Birthdays 23 July to 23 August)
2 January to 8 February, 16 April to 10 June, 18 September to 20 November

❀

Virgo (Birthdays 24 August to 23 September)
11 February to 1 April, 1 July to 18 September, 2 November to 19 December

❀

Libra (Birthdays 24 September to 23 October)
26 January to 1 April, 21 July to 15 September, 4 November to 26 December

❀

Scorpio (Birthdays 24 October to 22 November)
7 March to 11 May, 28 July to 17 September, 18 November to 19 December

❀

Sagittarius (Birthdays 23 November to 21 December)
11 January to 19 March, 12 June to 2 September, 11 November to 10 December

❀

Capricorn (Birthdays 22 December to 20 January)
8 January to 11 March, 11 May to 24 June, 20 September to 18 November

❀

Aquarius (Birthdays 21 January to 19 February)
21 January to 12 March, 10 May to 18 July, 1 October to 1 December

❀

Pisces (Birthdays 20 February to 20 March)
14 February to 19 April, 18 June to 17 August, 19 October to 8 December

Thunderball Astro-Guide for 2024

Thunderball forecasts are based on the power of the Sun and Jupiter in each zodiacal period. In a random draw there can be no guarantee, but these numbers may help to improve your chances. First, find your Sun sign in the left-hand column. Then read across the first panel to select five numbers 1–39 for the main part of your entry. Then select one number from the second panel for the Thunderball.

Sign	Dates	Main numbers						Thunderball			
ARIES	21 MARCH TO 20 APRIL	5	12	24	25	33	37	3	6	9	11
TAURUS	21 APRIL TO 21 MAY	14	26	28	31	34	36	2	7	10	13
GEMINI	22 MAY TO 21 JUNE	8	19	21	27	43	39	8	9	12	13
CANCER	22 JUNE TO 22 JULY	6	13	23	25	32	39	4	5	8	11
LEO	23 JULY TO 23 AUGUST	9	17	29	30	31	33	1	6	8	10
VIRGO	24 AUGUST TO 23 SEPTEMBER	8	19	27	30	33	36	3	5	7	13
LIBRA	24 SEPTEMBER TO 23 OCTOBER	13	22	26	29	36	38	1	3	6	9
SCORPIO	24 OCTOBER TO 22 NOVEMBER	8	15	16	26	28	35	4	10	11	13
SAGITTARIUS	23 NOVEMBER TO 21 DECEMBER	1	6	18	21	31	32	2	5	9	13
CAPRICORN	22 DECEMBER TO 20 JANUARY	14	24	28	33	35	36	3	6	8	10
AQUARIUS	21 JANUARY TO 19 FEBRUARY	5	8	15	30	31	37	1	3	4	13
PISCES	20 FEBRUARY TO 20 MARCH	8	13	17	20	27	33	2	4	5	11

THE SPELL LADY

35 years' experience

I can provide advice for white magik spells and rituals for romance, love, find a soul-mate, good luck, hex/curse removals, remote healing, and many more. Most things can be solved with a white magik spell.

Please contact me on: **01303 890942** or **07933 962544**

alstroud@btinternet.com

Your Lucky Lotto

The prevailing planetary influences are the basis for this astro-guide to lucky Lotto numbers in 2024. Any Lotto forecast must be fallible, but to give yourself the best chance of winning, refer to the section on your birth sign.

 ## ARIES

BORN 21 MARCH TO 20 APRIL

Aries is usually in a big rush to do things – impulsive is your middle name. Luckily, the spontaneous approach can work wonders now when playing the national lottery. If you normally use a fixed set of numbers, it may be worth trying the random approach this year. Chop and change your numbers for the next twelve months, but if you prefer not to do this, you could also try choosing digits associated with your personal finances and savings.

| 6 7 | 16 17 | 28 29 | 41 46 | 50 51 |
| 10 12 | 25 27 | 30 34 | 47 49 | 53 58 |

 ## TAURUS

BORN 21 APRIL TO 21 MAY

Jupiter – the planet of luck and opportunity – occupies your sign until May, putting you intuitively in touch with the Universe. This means that you are more receptive to what your heart and mind tells you – and this may have untold benefits for your play on the lottery. Consider choosing numbers connected to yourself, ones *exclusively* personal to you, for instance, your personal measurements or NHS/NI numbers.

| 2 6 | 14 18 | 24 25 | 32 34 | 52 54 |
| 10 11 | 21 22 | 27 28 | 40 45 | 57 58 |

 ## LEO

BORN 23 JULY TO 23 AUGUST

One of the 'money houses' on your solar chart is occupied by heavy-handed Saturn this year and this means you should probably aim for consistency in your approach to the lotto. Stay with any cherished favourite numbers and don't change them. Even if you're multiplying boards, keep to much the same ones on each. Numbers that are linked to your chosen career, your employer (or employees) or your mother are meaningful in 2024.

| 4 5 | 10 17 | 31 35 | 42 43 | 51 52 |
| 8 9 | 22 29 | 35 36 | 44 48 | 54 55 |

 ## VIRGO

BORN 24 AUGUST TO 23 SEPTEMBER

When it comes to the lottery for Virgo in 2024, making changes and sticking with them is the best way forward, especially if you've had any small victories lately. From May onwards, lucky Jupiter moves into the career area of your chart, and it will be onwards and upwards. This also means focusing on numbers connected with that area of your life. If you're not working at the moment, you could also try numbers associated with your parents.

| 2 4 | 11 12 | 26 27 | 35 37 | 48 50 |
| 8 9 | 22 23 | 30 33 | 38 42 | 51 52 |

 ## SAGITTARIUS

BORN 23 NOVEMBER TO 21 DECEMBER

It's an astrological cliché that Sagittarius is the luckiest sign, but if you want to make it even more true this year, look to those nearest to you. Your ruling planet, Jupiter, is having an impact on personal relationships from May onwards so if you've always played by yourself, it's time to go halves with a loved one. As an extra pointer to a lucky choice (up until May only) consider numbers linked to people you work with.

| 1 5 | 25 26 | 38 36 | 46 48 | 52 56 |
| 12 17 | 30 32 | 41 45 | 50 51 | 58 59 |

CAPRICORN

BORN 22 DECEMBER to 20 JANUARY

With powerful, life changing Pluto moving out of your sign this year you may find that you are able to see much more clearly ahead. In terms of lottery numbers, this means it's time to rip up the old and start anew – whether you usually choose numbers according to a system or play randomly, shake it up. New ones are the key! For the numbers themselves, consider choosing those associated with your profession or a club or group you belong to.

| 2 5 | 12 13 | 22 29 | 37 46 | 52 53 |
| 6 7 | 18 19 | 30 32 | 49 50 | 54 56 |

Astro-guide for 2024

Choose two numbers from the first square, then one number from each of the following squares. Either keep to the same numbers each week or vary the astrological indicators according to your personal vibrations.

USING THIS SYSTEM READER WINS £40,000 MRS THERESE SINGER OF GLASGOW

 ## GEMINI
BORN 22 MAY TO 21 JUNE

Jupiter – the planet of luck – visits Gemini from May through till the end of the year. This is likely to be the period when you'll feel more forward-looking and ambitious, and this might include a little gamble occasionally. If you are playing the lottery, consider varying your numbers – you never know when your superior intuition is at work! Alternatively, choose numbers linked to the recent past, especially those of significance during the last year.

4	9	19	22	34	36	43	44	51	52
11	14	26	30	37	39	45	47	53	56

CANCER
BORN 22 JUNE TO 22 JULY

Jupiter, the planet of luck and opportunity, allows you to correct many mistakes of the past this year – certainly from May onwards. This may also apply to how you play the lottery. If you have a strong feeling that there are certain numbers you *should* use, be open to it as your intuition is very powerful now. You could also try selecting numbers connected to friends in your social group or a hospital that is familiar to you.

7	9	20	22	29	30	36	40	48	51
12	17	23	27	32	33	46	47	56	59

 ## LIBRA
BORN 24 SEPTEMBER TO 23 OCTOBER

Trends reveal that Librans might benefit from taking a slightly selfish attitude to the lottery this year! With changeable, erratic Uranus in your house of joint finance, playing with others may become unreliable and an independent approach may be best. Lucky Jupiter also enters your house of foreign affairs from May, boosting your chances in the lotto. Try numbers connected with a holiday abroad, a university, or your partner's bank details.

6	8	12	13	28	29	40	41	50	56
9	10	17	19	32	38	44	48	57	59

 ## SCORPIO
24 OCTOBER TO 22 NOVEMBER

With the planet Jupiter in the relationship area of your solar chart this year, fortune could be on the rise if you play the lottery with a partner. Just let *them* select the numbers. Good things happen; in other words, through other people. Alternatively, when it comes to choosing the numbers themselves, personal relationships are your key – those that connect to your spouse, best friend or long-term partner (even in business) in particular.

2	3	12	14	20	27	40	41	46	48
4	9	16	17	36	38	43	45	52	53

 ## AQUARIUS
BORN 21 JANUARY TO 19 FEBRUARY

Pluto brings renewal and regeneration and it's moving through your sign in 2024, creating all kinds of radical changes in your life. Perhaps this may mean changes to your finances? Well, the name Pluto *is* synonymous with wealth, so who knows? Alter your numbers as much as you like for the first five months, then settle on the same ones. As for the numbers themselves, choose digits associated with your home and family or your partner.

1	7	11	16	22	23	32	33	44	49
8	9	18	19	25	29	35	41	55	59

 ## PISCES
BORN 20 FEBRUARY TO 20 MARCH

Saturn, the Lord of time and fate, occupies your sign during 2024, which means you should be consistent and plan for the long term. In terms of the lottery, it indicates that your best bet is to avoid the random approach and stay with a favourite six to twelve numbers. If you must change them, select digits from memorable phone numbers or those connected to local means of transport – buses, trains or your car.

4	8	13	16	28	30	39	40	44	47
9	10	18	23	31	38	41	42	54	56

Euro Millions Astro-indicator for 2024

Twelve has always been the perfect 'cyclical' number and is the 'pool' from which you can select from numbers below – they may help to improve your chances. Find your Sun sign in the left-hand column, then read across the first panel and choose five numbers (1–50) for the main board. Then, two for the Lucky Star section on the right. Some will overlap.

Sign	Dates	Main numbers								Lucky Stars			
ARIES	21 March to 20 April	4	7	10	11	27	29	40	44	3	6	10	13
TAURUS	21 April to 21 May	6	8	13	20	21	33	43	49	7	8	9	12
GEMINI	22 May to 21 June	3	9	13	26	36	39	44	50	1	5	6	12
CANCER	22 June to 22 July	5	6	20	23	38	39	40	48	3	7	9	11
LEO	23 July to 23 August	6	10	19	25	26	34	43	47	1	3	4	8
VIRGO	24 August to 23 September	1	8	16	17	28	30	43	50	2	5	6	9
LIBRA	24 September to 23 October	5	6	13	21	23	29	41	48	7	8	11	13
SCORPIO	24 October to 22 November	9	21	25	30	31	44	47	50	1	3	6	7
SAGITTARIUS	23 November to 21 December	4	9	13	20	26	34	45	46	1	4	5	7
CAPRICORN	22 December to 20 January	3	5	8	19	28	31	39	48	2	4	7	12
AQUARIUS	21 January to 19 February	3	9	14	26	35	42	43	44	6	10	11	13
PISCES	20 February to 20 March	6	14	15	24	25	40	41	45	1	8	9	12

gardening & planting by the mo•n 2024

Back by popular demand, Foulsham Publishing are proud to present this complete guide to gardening in harmony with the rhythm of the moon. Gardeners at RHS Wisley have proved the benefits of the lunar effect, which produces higher yields and better flavour in vegetables, and stronger, more colourful flower beds. Everything you need to know about the position of the moon and the planets through the year is here, plus a 15-month calendar and timetable.

£9.99

Published: September 2023

978-0-572-08439-6   30% discount on-line at www.foulsham.com or by calling 01256 302699 with code OM4.

Health Lottery Astro-guide for 2024

Health Lottery forecasts are based on the strength of Jupiter and planetary associations with the solar sixth house. These aspects are traditionally connected to health matters, whilst Jupiter signifies good luck generally. The numbers below may help to improve your chances at winning: just find your Sun sign, then select three numbers 1–50 from the first panel. Then choose two from the second 1–30.

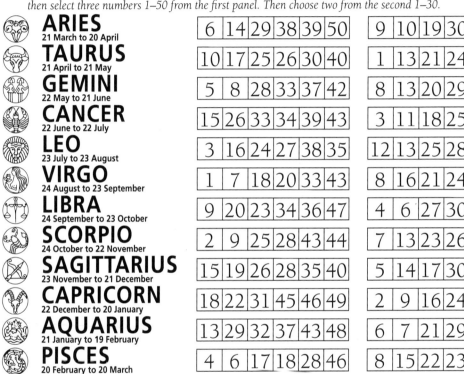

Sign	Dates	First panel						Second panel			
ARIES	21 March to 20 April	6	14	29	38	39	50	9	10	19	30
TAURUS	21 April to 21 May	10	17	25	26	30	40	1	13	21	24
GEMINI	22 May to 21 June	5	8	28	33	37	42	8	13	20	29
CANCER	22 June to 22 July	15	26	33	34	39	43	3	11	18	25
LEO	23 July to 23 August	3	16	24	27	38	35	12	13	25	28
VIRGO	24 August to 23 September	1	7	18	20	33	43	8	16	21	24
LIBRA	24 September to 23 October	9	20	23	34	36	47	4	6	27	30
SCORPIO	24 October to 22 November	2	9	25	28	43	44	7	13	23	26
SAGITTARIUS	23 November to 21 December	15	19	26	28	35	40	5	14	17	30
CAPRICORN	22 December to 20 January	18	22	31	45	46	49	2	9	16	24
AQUARIUS	21 January to 19 February	13	29	32	37	43	48	6	7	21	29
PISCES	20 February to 20 March	4	6	17	18	28	46	8	15	22	23

THE BEST
W🍷NES
IN THE
SUPER
MARKETS
2024

There are 30 wines rated a perfect 10
And 75 wines that are rated at 9...
Find out what they are and where to find them

NED HALLEY

978-0-572-04838-9

THE BEST WINES
IN THE SUPERMARKETS
Select the wine that suits your mood.

The top wine buyers are now in the supermarkets so that's where the most characterful wines are on offer. These tasting teams buy the pick of the world's vintages and offer a broad range of superb wines. This guide helps to direct your choice.
£9.99
Published: August 2023
30% discount on-line at www.foulsham.com or by calling 01256 302699 with code OM2.
Also available from good bookshops.

UK Fairs and Events 2024

Dates are based on traditional fixtures and both dates and venues are subject to change.
Always check local press, online or with the organisers well in advance.

AGRICULTURAL AND COUNTRYSIDE

Anglesey County Show: Gwalchmai 13–14 August

Appleby Horse Fair: Appleby-in-Westmorland, Cumbria 6–12 June

Bakewell Show: 7–8 August

Bingley Show: Myrtle Park, Bingley 20 July

Black Isle Show: Mansfield Showground, Muir of Ord 1 August

Border Union Show: Springwood Park, Kelso 26–27 July

Cheshire County Show: Tabley, Nr Knutsford 18–19 June

Country Fest: Westmorland County Showground, Lane Farm, Crooklands, Milnthorpe 1–2 June

Countryside Live: Great Yorkshire Showground, Harrogate 19–20 October

Cumberland County Show: Rickerby Park, Carlisle 8 June

Denbigh and Flint Show: The Green, Denbigh 15 August

Derbyshire County Show: Elvaston, Nr Derby 23 June

Devon County Show: Westpoint, Clyst St Mary, Exeter 16–18 May

Dorset County Show: Dorchester Showground 7–8 September

Dumfries and Lockerbie Agricultural Show: Park Farm, Dumfries 3 August

East of England Autumn Show: Showground, Peterborough 13 October

East of England Show and Just Dogs Live: Showground, Peterborough 5–7 July

Edenbridge and Oxted Agricultural Show: Ardenrun Showground, Lingfield 26 August

Eye Show: Goodrich Park, Palgrave 25–26 August

Great Yorkshire Show: Great Yorkshire Showground, Harrogate 9–12 July

Hertfordshire County Show: The Showground, Redbourn 25–26 May

Kelso Ram Sales: Springwood Park 13 September

Kent County Show: Detling, Maidstone 5–7 July (provisional)

Lincolnshire Show: Grange-de-Lings, Lincoln 19–20 June

Monmouthshire Show: Vauxhall Fields, Monmouth 29 August

Nantwich Show and International Cheese Awards: Dorfold Hall Park, Nantwich 31 July

New Forest and Hampshire County Show: New Park, Brockenhurst 23–25 July

Newark and Nottinghamshire County Show: Newark Showground, Newark-on-Trent 11–12 May

Newark Vintage Tractor and Heritage Show: Showground, Newark-on-Trent 9–10 November

North Somerset Show: Bathing Pond Fields, Wraxall, Nr Bristol 6 May

Northumberland County Show: Bywell, Nr Stocksfield 27 May

Oxfordshire County and Thame Show: Thame Showground 27 July

Pembrokeshire County Show: Withybush, Haverfordwest 20–22 August

Romsey Show: Broadlands, Romsey 14 September

Royal Bath & West AMES: Showground, Shepton Mallet 7 February

Royal Bath & West Dairy Show: Showground, Shepton Mallet 2 October

Royal Bath & West Show: Showground, Shepton Mallet 29 May–1 June (provisional)

Royal Cornwall Show: Wadebridge 6–8 June

Royal County of Berkshire Show: Newbury Showground 21–22 September

Royal Highland Show: Ingliston, Edinburgh 27–30 June (provisional)

Royal Norfolk Show: Norfolk Showground, Norwich 26–27 June

Royal Welsh Show: Llanelwedd, Builth Wells 12–25 July

Royal Welsh Winter Fair: Llanelwedd, Builth Wells 25–26 November

Shire Horse Society Spring Show: Arena UK Showground, Allington 15–17 March

Shropshire County Show: West Midlands Agricultural Showground, Shrewsbury 25 May

South of England Autumn Show and Game Fair: SoE Centre, Haywards Heath 28–29 September

South of England Show: South of England Centre, Ardingly, Haywards Heath 6–8 June (provisional)

Staffordshire County Show: Stafford Showground 29–30 May

Suffolk Show: Trinity Park, Ipswich 29–30 May

Surrey County Show: Stoke Park, Guildford 27 May

Tendring Hundred Show: Lawford House Park, Nr Manningtree 13 July

Turriff Show: The Showground, Turriff, Aberdeenshire 4–5 August

Westmorland County Show: Lane Farm, Crooklands 12 September

OTHER EVENTS

Badminton Horse Trials: 8–12 May

BBC Gardeners' World Live: NEC Birmingham 13–16 June (provisional)

Blackpool Illuminations: 1 September–1 January (provisional)

Border Union Championship Dog Show: Springwood Park, Kelso 15–16 June

Braemar Gathering: 7 September

Burghley Horse Trials: Burghley Park, Stamford 29 August–1 September

Chester Folk Festival: Kelsall 25–27 May

Cowes Week: 27 July–2 August

Crufts Dog Show: NEC Birmingham 7–10 March

Edinburgh International Festival: 2–25 August

Edinburgh Military Tattoo: Edinburgh Castle Esplanade 2–24 August

Glastonbury Festival: 26–30 June (provisional)

Golf. British Open Championship: Royal Troon 14–21 July. **Women's British Open**: St Andrews Date TBC. **Senior Open**: Royal Troon 25–28 July. For Amateurs, Boys and Girls Championships check www.randa.org

Hay Festival: Hay-on-Wye 23 May–2 June

Helston Furry Dance: 8 May

Henley Regatta: 25–30 June

The Hoppings (funfair): Town Moor, Newcastle 23–29 June

Horse Racing. Cheltenham Gold Cup: 15 March. **Grand National**: Aintree 13 April. **Scottish Grand National**: Ayr 20 April. **2000 Guineas**: Newmarket 4 May. **Epsom Derby**: 1 June. **Royal Ascot**: 18–22 June. **Glorious Goodwood**: 30 July–5 August. **St Leger**: Doncaster 14 September. **King George VI Chase**: Kempton 26 December.

Hull Fair: 4–12 October

Isle of Man TT Races: Douglas, IoM 27 May–8 June

Isle of Wight Festival: Seaclose Park, Newport, Isle of Wight 13–16 June

Jersey Battle of Flowers: 8 August

Leeds Festival: Bramham Park 23–25 August

Llangollen International Musical Eisteddfod: 3–7 July (provisional)

London to Brighton Veteran Car Run: Hyde Park, London–Madeira Drive, Brighton 3 November

London Harness Horse Parade: South of England Showground, Ardingly, Haywards Heath 1 April

London Marathon: Greenwich Park–The Mall, London 21 April

Lord Mayor's Show: City of London 9 November

Military Odyssey: Kent County Showground, Detling, Maidstone 24–26 August

Nottingham Goose Fair: October (dates unconfirmed; check local press)

Notting Hill Carnival: 25–26 August

'Obby 'Oss Day (May Day): Padstow, 1 May

Ould Lammas Fair: Ballycastle 26–27 August

Reading Festival: Richfield Avenue 23–25 August

RHS Chelsea Flower Show: 21–25 May (RHS members only first two days. Advance booking required.)

RHS Flower Show: Tatton Park, Nr Knutsford, Cheshire 17–21 July

RHS Hampton Court Palace Flower Show: 2–7 July (RHS members only first two days. Advance booking required.)

RHS Malvern Autumn Show: Three Counties Showground 20–22 September

RHS Malvern Spring Show: Three Counties Showground 9–12 May

Royal International Air Tattoo: RAF Fairford, Gloucestershire 12–14 July

Royal Windsor Horse Show: Home Park, Windsor (dates unconfirmed; check www.rwhs.co.uk)

Shrewsbury Folk Festival: 23–26 August

Shropshire County Horse Show: West Midlands Agricultural Showground, Shrewsbury 18 May

Sidmouth Folk Week: 2–9 August

Trooping the Colour: Horse Guards Parade, London 15 June

Three Choirs Festival: Worcester 27 July–3 August

Three Counties Championship Dog Show: Malvern Showground, Malvern 6–9 June

Three Counties Show: Three Counties Showground, Malvern 14–16 June

Up Helly Aa (fire festival and torchlight parade): Lerwick, Shetland Isles 30 January

Whitby Folk Festival: 25–30 August

Wimbledon Lawn Tennis Championships: 1–14 July

Lighting-up Times for 2024

Vehicle lamps must be used between sunset and sunrise. Times are in GMT, except 01.00 on 29 March to 01.00 on 25 October when they are BST (1 hour in advance). They are calculated for London (longitude 0°, latitude N.51°5).

Day	January h m	February h m	March h m	April h m	May h m	June h m	July h m	August h m	September h m	October h m	November h m	December h m
1	16 31	17 18	18 11	20 04	20 54	21 38	21 50	21 17	20 15	19 07	17 02	16 24
2	16 32	17 20	18 13	20 06	20 56	21 39	21 50	21 16	20 13	19 04	17 00	16 24
3	16 33	17 22	18 15	20 07	20 57	21 40	21 49	21 14	20 11	19 02	16 59	16 23
4	16 34	17 24	18 16	20 09	20 59	21 41	21 49	21 12	20 09	19 00	16 57	16 23
5	16 36	17 26	18 18	20 11	21 01	21 42	21 48	21 10	20 06	18 58	16 55	16 22
6	16 37	17 28	18 20	20 12	21 02	21 43	21 48	21 09	20 04	18 55	16 54	16 22
7	16 38	17 29	18 22	20 14	21 04	21 44	21 47	21 07	20 02	18 53	16 52	16 22
8	16 39	17 31	18 23	20 16	21 05	21 45	21 46	21 05	20 00	18 51	16 50	16 21
9	16 41	17 33	18 25	20 17	21 07	21 46	21 46	21 03	19 57	18 49	16 49	16 21
10	16 42	17 35	18 27	20 19	21 08	21 46	21 45	21 01	19 55	18 47	16 47	16 21
11	16 44	17 37	18 28	20 21	21 10	21 47	21 44	20 59	19 53	18 44	16 46	16 21
12	16 45	17 39	18 30	20 22	21 12	21 48	21 43	20 57	19 50	18 42	16 44	16 21
13	16 46	17 40	18 32	20 24	21 13	21 48	21 42	20 55	19 48	18 40	16 43	16 21
14	16 48	17 42	18 34	20 26	21 15	21 49	21 41	20 54	19 46	18 38	16 41	16 21
15	16 50	17 44	18 35	20 27	21 16	21 49	21 40	20 52	19 44	18 36	16 40	16 21
16	16 51	17 46	18 37	20 29	21 18	21 50	21 39	20 50	19 41	18 34	16 39	16 21
17	16 53	17 48	18 39	20 31	21 19	21 50	21 38	20 48	19 39	18 32	16 37	16 22
18	16 54	17 50	18 40	20 32	21 20	21 50	21 37	20 45	19 37	18 29	16 36	16 22
19	16 56	17 51	18 42	20 34	21 22	21 51	21 36	20 43	19 34	18 27	16 35	16 22
20	16 58	17 53	18 44	20 36	21 23	21 51	21 35	20 41	19 32	18 25	16 34	16 23
21	16 59	17 55	18 46	20 37	21 25	21 51	21 33	20 39	19 30	18 23	16 33	16 23
22	17 01	17 57	18 47	20 39	21 26	21 51	21 32	20 37	19 27	18 21	16 32	16 24
23	17 03	17 59	18 49	20 41	21 27	21 51	21 31	20 35	19 25	18 19	16 31	16 24
24	17 04	18 00	18 51	20 42	21 29	21 51	21 29	20 33	19 23	18 17	16 30	16 25
25	17 06	18 02	18 52	20 44	21 30	21 51	21 28	20 31	19 20	17 15	16 29	16 26
26	17 08	18 04	18 54	20 46	21 31	21 51	21 27	20 29	19 18	17 13	16 28	16 26
27	17 10	18 06	18 56	20 47	21 33	21 51	21 25	20 26	19 16	17 11	16 27	16 27
28	17 11	18 08	18 57	20 49	21 34	21 51	21 24	20 24	19 14	17 10	16 26	16 28
29	17 13	18 09	19 59	20 51	21 35	21 51	21 22	20 22	19 11	17 08	16 25	16 29
30	17 15		20 01	20 52	21 36	21 50	21 21	20 20	19 09	17 06	16 25	16 30
31	17 17		20 02		21 37		21 19	20 18		17 04		16 31

Make your holiday something extra special with the bestselling Brit Guides

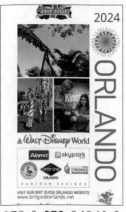

2024

ORLANDO

& WALT DISNEY World

Alamo · skypark · Gray Line · DRINKS

PARTNER SAVINGS

VISIT OUR BRIT GUIDE ORLANDO WEBSITE
www.britguideorlando.net

978-0-572-04840-2

Brilliant Days at DISNEYLAND PARIS

BRIT GUIDE RESEARCH TEAM

978-0-572-04699-6

For 30% discount, visit **www.foulsham.com** or call **01256 302699** and quote OM3 for Orlando or OM7 for Disneyland Paris. Also available from good bookshops. Ask for the latest edition when you order.